Quality Management Integration
in Long-Term Care

QUALITY MANAGEMENT INTEGRATION IN LONG-TERM CARE

Guidelines for Excellence

Maryjane G. Bradley, C.Q.M., C.Q.A., M.B.A.

and

Nancy R. Thompson, R.N.

HEALTH PROFESSIONS PRESS

Baltimore • London • Winnipeg • Sydney

Health Professions Press, Inc.
Post Office Box 10624
Baltimore, Maryland 21285-0624

www.healthpropress.com

Typesetting by AW Bennett, Inc., Hartland, Vermont.
Cover by XinaDesign, Baltimore, Maryland.
Printed in the United States of America by
Versa Press, Inc., East Peoria, Illinois.

Bulk discount purchase is available from the publisher by contacting Customer Service at 1-888-337-8808.

"Senior Executives' Nondelegable Roles" (p. 130) is used by permission of Harvard Business School Publishing Corporation.

"Data Collection—A 1-Minute Lesson" (p. 133) is © 1994 Briggs Corporation. To order a copy of *Continuous Quality Initiatives: A Manager's Guide* or any other Briggs Corporation products, call (800) 247-2343.

Library of Congress Cataloging-in-Publication Data
Bradley, Maryjane G.
    Quality management integration in long-term care : guidelines for excellence / Maryjane G. Bradley and Nancy R. Thompson.
        p.   cm.
    Includes bibliographical references and index.
    ISBN 1-878812-61-0
    1. Long-term care facilities—Quality control Handbooks, manuals, etc. 2. Long-term care of the sick—Quality control Handbooks, manuals, etc. I. Thompson, Nancy R. II. Title.
RA997.B69 1999
362.1′6′0685—dc21   99-27315
                                                                                                              CIP

CONTENTS

LIST OF EXHIBITS

PREFACE

Prior to the late 1980s, "long-term care" was primarily a range of services that were offered to frail older adults living in institutions that provided health care, personal care, and rehabilitation services, usually for extended periods of time. The contemporary emphasis on health restoration and returning elders to noninstitutional settings (e.g., individual's home, board and care home) forces facilities to respond to the growing expectations of health care professionals, regulatory and payer groups, family members, and residents. Quality management practices allow long-term care facilities to respond to environmental and industry changes, while enhancing responsiveness to customers. This responsiveness to change is a key factor in any facility's success.

The term "total quality management" (TQM) represents organization-wide quality improvement and quality management for all employees and managers in all departments and processes. Some organizations call the TQM process *continuous quality improvement* (CQI), referring to the steady changes in work processes that improve resident care and an organization's "bottom line." The focus of both CQI and TQM is providing service to an organization's customers by meeting their needs and requirements, delighting them with the services provided, and anticipating future needs. Because long-term care facilities vary widely in designating their quality management processes as TQM or CQI, we felt the need for a single designation—quality management integration, or QMI—that combines both philosophies and builds on their foundation.

QUALITY MANAGEMENT INTEGRATION (QMI)
QMI combines the concepts of TQM and CQI

Continuous quality improvement (CQI)
    Continuously improving the excellence of process outcomes/results to
    optimize customer satisfaction
Total quality management (TQM)
    Involving all parts of the organization and all of the employees in
    continuous process improvement

QMI addresses quality management issues such as

- Who is involved in QMI and in what areas of the organization?
- When and how does an organization implement QMI practices?
- What is the best way to improve an organization's work processes?
- What is the intended effect on customers?
- How does an organization set priorities?

The two primary questions that are addressed in this book are

1. How can we improve long-term care for each resident, while simultaneously becoming more effective throughout the facility as a whole?
2. How can we be more efficient and reduce the risk of error, yet maintain our focus on the customer satisfaction of each resident and his or her family?

Because the concepts and outcomes of TQM and CQI are so closely related, we developed the QMI model and its six core concepts. Each of the six concepts is founded on data collection and analysis, as described in Chapter 1 (see the QMI model at the beginning of each chapter). We stress *integration* in QMI because the core concepts and their reliance on data are integrated into the daily work of the entire organization and do not stand alone as a separate quality project.

Applying the six core concepts of QMI is vital for successful strategic planning, training/education, and implementation. Because we take a realistic approach to implementation, barriers and critical issues are identified and defined clearly, as are "real-world" suggestions on working through obstacles. Powerful QMI tools and techniques are detailed to ensure that teams and individual employees or managers will be successful, whether initiating strategic planning for quality improvement or improving an established process. The 3-phase quality management integration process (p. 15 and Chapter 3 show this process in detail) ensures that leadership activities, such as the organization's quality council, are effective.

An actual case study in long-term care—Woodland Care Center at the beginning of its quality journey—is introduced and followed through the book. (Woodland Care Center is a pseudonym that is used to protect the true identity of the facility. Most of the other mini-cases are synthesized from the authors' combined experiences in long-term care.) Woodland's journey reflects many critical issues and barriers that must be faced by other LTC organizations and illustrates the QMI process.

Each chapter contains displays that highlight the human or practical aspects of QMI implementation in long-term care facilities. There are numerous illustrations of implementation procedures and various case materials are included.

Chapter 1 provides an overview of the six core concepts that are involved in implementing an effective QMI process and illustrates their reliance on data-driven decision making. These six concepts make up what we call the QMI model. Each core concept is described in detail and is accompanied by practical implementation guidelines for their integration in daily work. A number of key terms and techniques are introduced, including the 3-phase quality management integration process. This process is a guide through the quality journey.

Next, we describe the issues that are faced by the long-term care industry within the broader history of TQM and CQI. Chapter 2 examines the roots of quality management and its development in other service industries and in the health care industry. Successful techniques as well as potential pitfalls in introducing QMI to a facility are highlighted. Issues such as customer service; management's role in implementing quality management processes; and data collection and analysis, or management by fact, are discussed. We include two mini-cases that demonstrate the implementation of QMI principles. The cases illustrate both the impressive cost savings and the customer satisfaction improvements that are possible through QMI.

In Chapter 3, we describe the application of the 3-phase quality management integration process at Woodland Care Center. The Woodland case also demonstrates the use of a number of successful techniques and tools that are critical to QMI implementation. Detailed examples are drawn from activities at Woodland. Instead of adding complex work systems, we explore how QMI can make work processes more efficient for staff, while improving resident and family satisfaction.

Chapters 4 and 5 are central to our discussion of quality management in long-term care: They help address the question, what barriers and critical issues within the facility and in the broader long-term care environment might you face as your organization implements QMI? Chapter 4 explores in detail the potential barriers and critical issues that are internal to long-term care facilities and strongly affect the success of QMI implementation in them. The potential roadblocks to implementing QMI range from short-term focus and resource limitations to turf wars and ineffective communication. The issues that are critical to successful implementation of QMI include the pivotal role of management, how to gain support from physicians, the family as a system, and the corporate or multi-facility viewpoint about QMI.

Chapter 5 explores potential barriers and critical issues that are external to the long-term care facility. We examine powerful drawbacks of the current system, in particular the regulatory requirements and financial reimbursement structures in long-term care. We believe that the contemporary emphasis on meeting standards rather than exceeding them promotes quality *assurance*, not quality *improvement*, and inhibits cost-containment efforts unintentionally. In addition, we explore the decisive impact of financial reimbursement systems and regulatory requirements on policy and proposed process changes in health care.

A section in Chapter 5 focuses on integrated delivery systems (IDSs; e.g., networks, mergers, managed care organizations) and addresses the complexity of future health care systems. In many facilities IDSs have forced profound changes in systems and care processes. If problems exist in free-standing local facilities, imagine how those problems can be compounded in merged networks. The six core concepts of QMI and the tools of data collection and analysis enable managed care organizations to

- Limit risk
- Provide cost-effective services
- Measure customer satisfaction
- Track the success of residents' long-term clinical outcomes
- Provide residents' continuum of care across an integrated health care system

Chapter 6 covers the crucial role that data collection and analysis play in QMI and considers the data collected during Woodland's quality project and in several mini-cases. Tracking levels and trends in long-term care data and measuring both your work processes and your results are fundamental to management-by-fact QMI processes. Sets of key quality indicators and several mini-cases illustrate the application of QMI tools and concepts to everyday issues in long-term care facilities. There is an emphasis on analyzing and studying long-term data across multiple resident groups as well as on studying individual residents to monitor changes in clinical and functional effectiveness. The usefulness and interpretation of satisfaction survey data for both customers and employees also are considered.

Finally, Chapter 7 pulls together the quality management principles and issues that must be addressed to integrate QMI successfully into your organization's daily work. Issues to be addressed by QMI leaders are detailed, and the training and certification of quality managers are discussed. Working with both internal and external quality consultants also is examined. Appendixes A–M provide QMI implementation tools and other reference materials.

We have combined two voices in this book, an internal and an external consultant. One of the authors is a vice president of organizational performance who works full time in a large, multifacility organization; the other author is an external consultant who supports long-term care organizations for a specific project or for a specified period of time, bringing an "outsider's" fresh viewpoint and breadth of experience to the issues that surround a QMI process. Our tasks are very similar, even if our daily professional lives appear different: We both provide support and consultation to organizations that are struggling with the communication problems and critical issues that surround every QMI implementation in long-term care. Thus, our visions of the outcomes of successful QMI processes are parallel in most applications.

The variety of our professional experiences comes into use during each QMI implementation project as management and staff groups face QMI's culture changes, the need for enhanced communication, and the shifts in job roles. We communicate the "win-win" benefits for every individual. Our confidence in QMI derives from seeing successful organizations transformed as they provide better service to their customers and clients and from working with organization leaders to develop efficient work processes and ever-improving employee satisfaction.

About the Authors

Maryjane G. Bradley, C.Q.M., C.Q.A., M.B.A., has been a quality management consultant (both internal and external consulting) since 1985. She has supported health care delivery in the long-term care industry, service organizations such as airlines, projects in nonprofit organizations, and manufacturing companies. She holds degrees from Radcliffe College and Metropolitan State University and is certified as a quality manager (CQM) and a quality auditor (CQA) through the American Society for Quality.

Ms. Bradley has served as a Certified Master Examiner in a number of organizations through the annual Minnesota Quality Awards since 1992. She has conducted numerous presentations of statistical process management techniques and train-the-trainer concepts at regional and national conferences.

As adjunct faculty in the Minneapolis area, she has taught at both Metropolitan State University and Century College. She is a member of the American Society for Quality, the Quality Improvement Network for Long-Term Care and Seniors, and the Council of Independent Professional Consultants.

Nancy R. Thompson, R.N., has worked in health care for more than 20 years, especially in the areas of human resources and organizational development; almost half of her career has been spent as an internal quality consultant. She is Vice President of Organizational Performance for Ebenezer Society, a multifacility long-term care organization that is part of Fairview Health Services in Minneapolis. At Ebenezer, she is responsible for facilitating the implementation and maintenance of the quality management process and for integrating the QMI philosophy into day-to-day operations.

Ms. Thompson has worked in for-profit, nonprofit, and government-owned long-term care organizations from the perspective of frontline care provider, supervisor, and middle and senior management. She constantly draws on this experience as she supports staff and managers who face rapid changes in long-term care and health care delivery systems. She also has provided consultation and training to professional organizations, acute and long-term health care organizations, colleges, universities, and community groups.

Thompson has authored articles in *PROVIDER*, the professional journal of the American Health Care Association, and *Nursing Home* magazine. She is a member of numerous professional societies including the Association for Quality and Participation, the American Society for Training and Development, and the Quality Improvement Network for Long-Term Care and Seniors.

ACKNOWLEDGMENTS

We are very grateful to the professional colleagues who recommended various improvements in our early drafts of this book and in some of the QMI tools and models that we have developed. We definitely approve of continuous quality improvement, in our book as well as our work lives.

The kind reviewers who offered their expertise in our preparation process included Cathy Bergland, R.M.T., L.N.H.A., Director of Quality Management, Presbyterian Homes of Minnesota; Vivian Booker, M.H.A., Facility Administrator; Mary Chapa, R.N., Director of Operations, Fairview Home Care Services; Margie Kissner, Director of Performance Improvement, Ebenezer Social Ministries; Theresa A. Lang, R.N., CDONA, Senior Health Services Consultant, Specialized Medical Services, Inc.; Bob Manske, M.P.H., Vice President of Quality Improvement, Walker Methodist, Inc.; Glenn Widmark, Associate Administrator, Covenant Village of Cromwell; and Thomas Stofac, Vice President, Senior Care System Planning and Development, Fairview Health Services.

Many colleagues in other training and consulting settings have shared their insights as well—to all of you our heartfelt thanks.

KEY CONCEPTS IN QUALITY MANAGEMENT INTEGRATION

This chapter provides an overview of the six core concepts of quality management integration (QMI) and demonstrates their reliance on data analysis. The QMI model (see above) provides a framework for the ideas presented in subsequent chapters. This chapter also introduces "Woodland Care Center," a fictional long-term care facility that serves here as a model for strategic planning and implementation of QMI. QMI activities at Woodland are grouped to illustrate the phases of the 3-phase quality management integration model. In addition, several ways of evaluating the success of a QMI implementation are illustrated.

Long-term care facilities are on the crest of a new wave. With payers, regulators, and consumers demanding effective, efficient care and services, facility leaders must rethink the traditional way of managing. The mindset used to operate a health care facility requires giving careful attention to the expectations of all customers, along with the flexibility to meet changing needs.

This book addresses the organization-wide transformation that is needed to sustain competitiveness in a rapidly changing environment. By integrating a quality management philosophy that the authors have developed—QMI—organizations have been able to create a culture in which employees are empowered to deliver the kind of care and services that enlightened customers demand. Creating this environment is not easy, however. Pitfalls and barriers abound on the road to quality management, not the least of which is simply the way that people think. Each person brings to the work environment a set of mental models that is shaped by life experience. Mental models shape perceptions. For example, if management believes that the facility operates best by setting up specific departments to perform specific functions and that those functions should be carried out in a manner that maximizes the efficiency of the individual department, then the result will be departments competing against one another for resources. When every department manager is working to optimize only his or her own department, often the facility as a whole suffers.

A long-term care facility cannot afford departments and people competing against one another. Progress occurs only when people work together toward a common vision. The transformation to total quality begins with the recognition that the whole is greater than the sum of its parts. In other words, the process of ensuring and delivering high-quality care should be straightforward and easily understood. It should not be a barrier to staff success. A good example of this concept is detailed in the following, told to the authors by a former nursing assistant:

> Last year, I started working as a nursing assistant at a local nursing facility. I remember feeling very excited about caring for the residents and believing that I could really make a difference in their lives. In orientation I was told that my first priority was to give good care to the residents. The staff development director told my orientation class that "the residents come first" and that we should do everything we can to make them feel comfortable. She spoke of the facility's commitment to quality and the quality management integration process. She said that as the primary caregivers, we were empowered to ensure quality care and service to our customers. After being inspired by these words, I was frustrated to find that when I got out on the floor, there were many barriers that made it very difficult to give good-quality resident care.
>
> When I got to work each morning, I would get my assignment from the nurse and then walk to the clean linens room to gather the linens I would need to care for my residents. Upon opening the door, what do you think I found? *Nothing*. Nothing except for a few draw sheets and maybe a couple of pillowcases. How could I bathe my residents and change their beds if I didn't have linens?
>
> After a few days of this, I got smart. I figured out a way to have the necessary linens available to ensure that my residents received good care. When linens were delivered to the nursing units in the late morning, I would store a supply of washcloths, towels, and sheets in a little hiding place I found. Then those linens would be available to use the next morning. Sure enough, it worked. I had what I needed for my residents. I felt good about my ability to put the residents first and to give them the care they deserved. Then one day, the director of nursing came storming down the hall, pointed her finger at me, and said angrily, "I caught you hoarding linens—I'm writing you up!" I didn't understand. I was expected to give high-quality care to my residents, but when I did everything in my power to do just that, I got shot down. I felt frustrated, guilty, angry, and very demoralized.

Guidelines for Excellence in Care and Service

Six core concepts combine to form the philosophical beliefs and values of the QMI model. Because these concepts are presented as strategic approaches to QMI, each core

QMI concept is accompanied by implementation guidelines to lead the administrator or quality professional toward an effective QMI process. A description of these core beliefs is provided along with some specific actions that facility leaders can use to integrate quality management. Together these core concepts combine the powerful philosophy of total quality management (TQM) with the process of continuous quality improvement (CQI) to create organizational excellence.

In every QMI core concept, decisions are driven by data, both process and outcomes data.

$$\text{Data} \rightarrow \text{Information} \rightarrow \text{Knowledge} \rightarrow \text{Action}$$

Process measures keep quality professionals alerted to the efficiency of work processes (e.g., timeliness of tray delivery), and outcome measures permit the analysis of the process' effectiveness or end results (e.g., resident satisfaction with meal service). The driving force behind successful problem solving and decision making in any of the core concepts is the effective use of data. Data alone are meaningless unless they are analyzed and turned into information. Information must then be turned into knowledge from which leaders are able to make decisions and take action.

Although each of the QMI core concepts is discussed separately, the concepts are interrelated and interdependent. Focusing on any one of the core concepts to the exclusion of the others usually leads to frustration and disappointment for both managers and staff.

Core Concept 1: Customer Focus

The foundation of quality management is understanding who the customer is and then meeting and exceeding customer expectations. Nursing facilities provide their products and services to four external customer groups: residents; families and designated caregivers, who often make decisions for residents; regulatory agencies; and payer groups, such as insurance companies or government agencies. These external customers are referred to as the *four customer groups* throughout this book. *External customers* are not employees of the long-term care organization.

Services also are extended to *internal customers*. They are organization personnel who receive information, services, or other professional support from fellow employees. In this way they are each other's customers because they work together to serve the four external customer groups. The results of the work processes performed by the internal customers make up the products or services that are provided to residents, families, payer groups, and regulatory agencies. Facility staff also form relationships with providers of care outside the facility, such as discharge planners, nurse practitioners, physicians, and pharmacy personnel. The effectiveness of these relationships has a powerful effect on quality outcomes. Providers need to nurture these relationships. Both external and internal customers should be treated with courtesy, helpfulness, and efficiency.

Customer focus in the QMI model details the importance of external customer relationships and response. When customers are mentioned in this section, the reference is specifically to the four external customer groups.

A unique aspect of long-term care is that unlike customers in other industries, residents frequently have no say whether they will purchase or pay for the facility's services. Many times, others make these decisions for them.

The QMI concept describes employee and management involvement in the continuous improvement of all processes and services to provide quality goods and services to all internal customers and to the four external customer groups.

Customer Focus Implementation Guidelines

1. Develop a clear definition of the word *customer*; for example, "Customers are defined as anyone to whom a product, service, or information is provided."
2. Communicate the facility's mission and customer focus. For example, this information can be
   ◆ Provided to all new residents and families during the admission process
   ◆ Shared with potential employees during the interview process
   ◆ Presented to new employees during the orientation process
   ◆ Reinforced with current employees
   ◆ Incorporated into promotional materials
3. Communicate the facility's mission and customer focus to contracted suppliers who serve customers on its behalf. The information can be stated in all contracts and/or contract negotiations with vendors, subcontractors, and members of partnerships.
4. Provide customers with information and education about the care and services provided, as well as how they can contact the organization's leadership to share their ideas and concerns.
5. Incorporate accountability for the practice of positive customer relations in all job descriptions and performance evaluations, including those for managers and supervisors.
6. Share customer feedback (both positive and negative) with employees.
7. Develop improvement plans that are based on customer feedback.
8. Create a system to respond to customer concerns or complaints.
9. Create a system to collect and analyze data regarding both internal and external customer expectations and satisfaction with care and services; for example, written surveys, telephone surveys, focus groups, one-to-one conversations, comment cards, and resident and/or family council meetings.

Core Concept 2: Continual Learning

To ensure the delivery of quality care and service, employees must possess the knowledge, skills, and abilities to perform their jobs competently. The facility's hiring and orientation processes as well as ongoing training must be designed to ensure that employees gain and maintain these skills and are given opportunities to advance their knowledge and skill levels. A facility that embraces QMI uses many resources for continual learning and draws on the knowledge, perspectives, and experiences of all staff members to improve the products and services provided to customers.

Continual Learning Implementation Guidelines

1. Design the facility's staff development program to support organizational strategies and goals.
2. Provide potential employees with an overview of the facility's mission, vision, and quality management philosophy during the recruitment and selection processes.
3. Acquaint all new employees with the facility's quality management philosophy.
4. Incorporate QMI principles in all aspects of the employees' daily work during job-specific training. This is quality management *integration*.
5. Assess the educational needs and the strengths of employees. At the time the person is hired, determine his or her orientation needs and then continually assess the learning needs so that appropriate training and education programs are offered to upgrade and reinforce skills and provide professional or personal growth.
6. Provide a follow-up orientation within 1–4 months of employment start date to evaluate the progress and identify further training needs of new employees.
7. Encourage cross-training to broaden employee understanding of facility systems and activities. Cross-training improves efficiency and provides future career path options for employees.
8. Allocate time for employees to attend continuing education programs.
9. Ensure that staff developers possess adequate training and communication skills and an understanding of QMI principles.
10. Create an environment that promotes continual learning, in which learning is considered a job expectation, learning opportunities and resources are made available to all employees, forums exist to share what is learned, and learning is recognized or rewarded.
11. Create a system to collect and analyze data that measure participation in and successful implementation of training and learning activities.

Core Concept 3: Employee Involvement

In a successful QMI environment the role of the manager changes from directing, organizing, and controlling to coordinating, supporting, coaching, and mentoring. Managers recognize that the people who have the greatest expertise regarding a process are the people who actually work within that process. Therefore, solving process problems or improving a process requires involvement from those closest to it, usually the direct care and service providers. This is called "employee involvement."

The Power of Participative Management

Quality care and services are the result of the work of a team of competent individuals who are committed to taking care of the customer. Employee commitment cannot be forced. Commitment is a feeling that comes from working in an environment that promotes positive relationships and a high level of trust. Most people come to work each day wanting to do the best job that they can. When people do not provide good care and service, the question becomes not what is wrong with them but what are the barriers standing in their way. In participative management, employees participate in making decisions about process improvements and in solving problems. High-quality care and service happens when people have what they need to do their best work, including the following:

- Clear direction
- Knowledge, skills, and information
- Involvement in problem solving and decision making
- Tools and resources
- Support from supervisor and team members

A manager's job is to provide employees with the direction and support they need to be successful in their jobs and to remove any barriers that interfere with their ability to satisfy customers. Through a participative management style, managers create a motivating environment that generates a feeling of commitment and empowers employees to grow and develop into peak performers.

It is helpful to consider how managers and staff view their own roles. The assumptions—conscious and unconscious—that people make determine their beliefs, and beliefs determine behaviors. Because an individual's first management lessons came from his or her parents, many managers adopt a parental view, and thus a parental style, of management.

The Parental View of Management

Parental managers believe that the success of the department or facility is on their shoulders. They assume that their role is to be in control and to handle any problems that arise. Their motto is "The buck stops here." The consequence of parental management is employees who become passive and accept less responsibility. A more effective way to view the managerial role is to understand the relationship between supervisor and employee as a partnership.

The Partnership View of Management

Managers who view their role as a partnership between them and their employees recognize the knowledge and skills that each employee brings to the workplace. In partnerships, managers work to encourage shared responsibility in producing efficient and effective care and service. Through this type of leadership, employees participate in planning and problem solving by sharing their understanding of the situation, contributing their knowledge and skills, and offering ideas for improvement.

Employee Involvement Implementation Guidelines

1. Promote an environment of cooperation and collaboration in which employees are empowered to perform at their highest level in an atmosphere of teamwork and trust. This environment is one of participative management.
2. Establish communication systems that are open and inclusive and are aimed at reducing ambiguity and promoting healthy working relationships.
3. Give employees the support and direction that they need to perform their jobs effectively.

4. Structure jobs in ways that promote quality of work life. This includes providing the following:
    ◆ Involvement in problem solving and decision making
    ◆ Ongoing positive and constructive feedback
    ◆ Opportunities for growth and development
    ◆ Support from supervisors and team members
    ◆ Opportunities to use creativity and humor
    ◆ Safe working conditions
5. Hold both employees and management accountable for fostering an environment that demonstrates the value of workforce diversity.
6. Create a system to collect and analyze data that measure employee satisfaction and participation in continuous improvement activities.

Core Concept 4: Systems Orientation

A system is a group of processes that work together to produce a common product or service outcome. Long-term care services are made up of a number of systems with interdependent parts or functions, all having the same mission: to meet the needs and exceed the expectations of customers. Just as the human body is made up of a number of systems, such as the skeletal, the circulatory, and the respiratory systems, the long-term care facility functions through the coordination of the many processes within the admissions system, the meal service system, the resident care planning system, and many others. The facility's administration seeks to enhance the performance of the entire system rather than just the performance of individual processes or individual departments.

A systems orientation requires thinking about the way that work gets done. For example, for the admissions system to work well, all of the departments involved must make admissions a positive experience for the customer. Creating a positive experience requires that the various departments know how to work together to ensure that the work is flowing smoothly and that there are no unnecessary delays in the resident's getting settled in his or her new environment.

Systems Orientation Implementation Guidelines

1. Identify key organizational systems (i.e., interdepartmental systems) and the individual processes that they include. Make a flowchart and document these key processes. Communicate their importance to all staff to ensure that staff focus on these organizational priorities.
2. Ensure that the facility's systems are designed to provide a comfortable, seamless experience for customers.
3. Establish communication systems to optimize information sharing, mutual learning, and problem solving through the use of multiple communication methods.
4. Ensure that employees have access to the tools, equipment, and resources that are necessary to perform their jobs effectively.
5. Promote cooperation and collaboration between individuals and departments. Cooperation removes the competition for resources and recognition between departments and divisions. Accomplish this by making customer needs central in importance. Customer needs are the primary drivers for change.

6. Monitor changes in the health care environment. Anticipate changes in customer needs and initiate necessary responses in the facility's internal systems to meet their demands.
7. Establish systems to communicate expectations to suppliers and methods to evaluate whether these expectations are being met (often, systems begin outside organizations, with suppliers or vendors).
8. Create a system to collect and analyze data that measure the ongoing process and outcomes of each of the key organizational systems, for example, admissions system, medication administration system, and preventive maintenance system. Track key indicators through the organization for continuous improvement and quality management.

Core Concept 5: Continuous Process Improvement

To continuously improve, organizations must analyze their work processes and reduce unnecessary or repeated steps. Not only does this result in improved quality of products and services but it also increases efficiency, so that people can work smarter, not harder. A systematic and scientific approach to improvement is used to continually improve and control work processes. In addition, all employees must seek new and innovative ways of meeting customers' needs and even exceeding their expectations.

Virtually everything that is done in a long-term care facility is a process. What a process looks like must be understood before improvements can be made. The display on page 9 illustrates the process of transforming an organization's resources *(inputs)* into process results *(outputs)*.

Many of the inputs that go into long-term care processes come from external suppliers. For example, food used to prepare meals, medical supplies and equipment, and cleaning products come from outside vendors. In addition, facilities often contract with other organizations to provide services to residents, such as rehabilitation therapies, dietary services, and laboratory services. In these cases steps in the process flow begin outside the facility's walls, perhaps with initial negotiations. It is to the facility's advantage to establish effective relationships with vendors in which trust and a sense of partnership exist between the facility and the supplier. The facility must implement a method to communicate expectations to suppliers and to ensure that those expectations are met. When inputs to a process are defective or inadequate, the entire process can fail. In some cases suppliers may have established a comprehensive approach to quality management and improvement within their organizations. If so, the supplier may be a resource and perhaps a powerful ally for facility leaders as they pursue their quality journey.

To be *systematic,* a quality improvement process continuously tracks key processes on a regular basis; organizations establish an agreed-on process flow that is followed by all individuals and monitored at regular intervals. They ensure that continuous process improvement is accomplished systematically. A process problem that develops consistently at certain locations in the process flow is referred to as a *process bottleneck*. Like the narrow neck of a bottle, the problem slows the speed of what flows through it. For example, in long-term care a process bottleneck may occur in distributing medicines or assessing the needs of new residents. Process bottlenecks must be identified and resources applied to them. Improving process bottlenecks reflects a systems orientation because it maintains the flow of

Transforming Inputs (*Resources*) into Outputs (*Services and Products*)

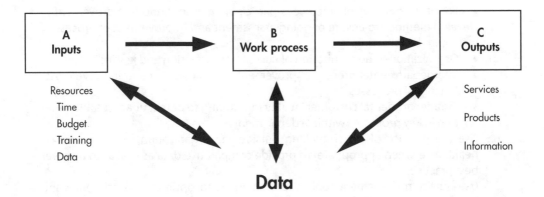

A **Inputs** in the process of making a bed include
  • A person to do the work
  • Linens
  • The bed itself
  • A method or procedure for making the bed
B The **work process** occurs when the person making the bed completes each step of the bed-making process, using available inputs/resources to accomplish the work.
C The **output** of this process is a correctly made bed—a bed that is outfitted with clean linens and that looks neat. It helps to provide a pleasant environment for the customer (resident) who resides in the room.

Data may be collected during all three steps of the process flow to analyze the performance of either the work or the results.

products, services, and information through the organization. (Additional information can be found in Goldratt.[1,2])

Within cross-functional systems, in which several processes join together, individual departments should be aware of the effect of their process improvements on other processes or departments. A systems orientation, the particular role of management, maintains focus on improving the organization as a whole (Core Concept 4). It is important to understand the relationship between systems and processes. Changing one department's process may have a significant impact on other processes in the same system. The display on page 10 illustrates this concept well.

Continuous Process Improvement Implementation Guidelines

1. Involve employees in the continuous improvement of quality, including resolving existing problems, implementing process improvement ideas, and seeking innovative methods for delivering care and service.
2. Include an expectation of employees' participating in QMI in all job descriptions.
3. Provide employees and management with basic and ongoing education related to quality management concepts and tools.
4. Establish a system to foster suggestions and ideas for process improvement. The system should include the following:
   ◆ Acknowledgment of the idea

- ◆ Communication to originator regarding follow-through
- ◆ Participation of originator in follow-through when appropriate
- ◆ Formal recognition of employees' participation in continuous improvement
5. Develop methods to ensure ongoing assessment and improvement of processes, including the following:
   - ◆ Organization-wide monitoring of customer satisfaction and key indicators
   - ◆ Interdepartmental process improvement teams to study and improve cross-functional processes
   - ◆ Intradepartmental customer/quality monitoring to detect unacceptable variation in key processes within a department
6. Use the practice of benchmarking outside the organization (perhaps outside health care, when appropriate) to provide comparative data as well as to discover best practices.
7. Use quality management tools and techniques to optimize the efficiency and effectiveness of processes and to promote high-quality outcomes.
8. Evaluate managers on the extent to which they encourage and support employee involvement in continuous improvement efforts.
9. Celebrate improvement successes.

Processes and Systems: Doing Your Work

Processes: Transforming inputs (*resources*) into outputs (*services and products*)

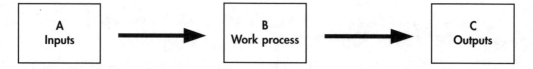

Processes are often the focus of departments or employees. When something goes wrong, blame the *process*, not the *person*.

Systems: Interrelated processes, all focused on reaching the same outcomes (*services and products*)

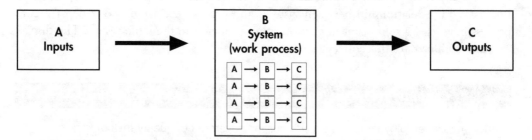

Systems are the particular focus of organizational leadership and the QMI effort.

Notes: QMI focuses on optimizing each system as a whole, not as its individual components such as separate processes, which may compete for resources.

Organizational leadership sets overall priorities, based on long- and short-term strategic plans and using prioritization techniques.

The biggest opportunities for cost savings and quality improvement lie in the system. Special focus should be setup times, waste, delays, and rework within individual processes.

10. Create a system to collect and analyze data that measure supplier services. Include data related to supplier and customer needs and outcomes in process improvement planning.
11. Collect and analyze data to determine patterns and trends, to prioritize improvement efforts, and to generate ideas for innovations.

Core Concept 6: Leadership

Leadership is the driving force behind all of the core concepts. For successful QMI implementation within an organization's existing culture, facility leaders must discover and implement new ways of thinking, guiding, directing, and solving problems. The management team must not only understand the core concepts of QMI but also actually model roles and behaviors consistent with these principles. Leadership is the foundation that supports all of the other guidelines. Unless and until senior staff and executives are involved actively in QMI, success will be limited at best.

Leadership Implementation Guidelines

1. Recognize that QMI leadership involves all senior managers and executives, who will spearhead the necessary changes in the corporate culture. For example, leadership plays a central role in communications, strategic planning, improvement of managerial procedures and systems, and transformation of expectations and standards in the organization. (*Note:* The same implementation guidelines apply to the individual department or work area as well, but QMI leadership at senior levels accelerates the transformation process.)
2. Create and participate in an infrastructure that supports the integration of quality management. A quality council or other committee or group should guide QMI efforts.
3. Develop a quality management plan that clearly defines a system for identifying, prioritizing, and resolving quality issues. (See Appendix L for a sample plan.)
4. Send the clear message that delivery of high-quality care and service is a priority in all activities of the organization. Put quality issues first on all meeting agendas.
5. Define standards of quality care and service based on customer expectations. Ensure that all processes include standards and that standards are communicated to all of the employees.
6. Establish systems to measure, evaluate, and communicate success in meeting or exceeding identified standards.
7. Establish systems that formally recognize employees' contributions to the QMI process.
8. Allocate resources (e.g., human, financial, information) to support the facility's quality management initiative.
9. Encourage the use of pilot projects to test proposed solutions and hasten implementation of improved processes. Risk occasional failures to gain a broad spectrum of successes.
10. Develop and use a strategic plan that considers both the external health care environment and the strengths and weaknesses of the internal environment to create actionable strategies for the facility's future.

11.   Base strategic planning and management decisions on data that have been collected and analyzed.

Successful QMI depends on leadership that understands the power of each of the core concepts and how they interact. Without this understanding, facility and corporate managers may get caught in a continuous cycle of reacting to crises:

> I'm the director of nursing, and I'm at the end of my rope. We've been told by the corporate office that we have to implement this quality management integration program, and I have no idea where I'm going to find the time! Right now I'm trying to hire more nursing assistants because our new ones keep quitting. I guess we're just not hiring the right kind of people to do this job. They seem okay when they go through orientation, but when they get on the floor they just fall apart! Not only that, the state surveyors are due any day. I'm worried about our meal service because we were cited on that last year. I thought I had the problems fixed, but the same problems seem to be cropping up again to haunt me. I guess I'm going to have to start writing people up again to get them in line.
>   Quality Management Integration—I don't know why we have to start this program. We've always given the best quality care in our facility! How could QMI possibly help us here?

In a successful QMI process the leaders' decisions are based on knowledge and confirmed with facts. Data (facts) are used to determine improvement priorities and to support process changes. Staff members are involved in collecting and analyzing the data to make good decisions and to measure whether process improvements were successful. It is important that data not be used to blame individuals or departments for performance problems. Adopting a nonblaming continuous improvement philosophy is one of the most fundamental shifts required by QMI leadership.

QMI efforts in an individual department or work area result in benefits, but these benefits increase dramatically when quality management processes are integrated by senior leadership in all facility processes and systems. In a facility that employs fully integrated quality management, leaders demonstrate respect for the dignity, knowledge, and potential contributions of all staff members. Leaders create an environment in which people can be innovative and can experience joy in their work.

Using Data Aligns QMI Efforts with Organization's Priorities

Data are at the heart of the QMI model and provide its strength in process and system changes. Selecting process improvement priorities and indicators employs facts and figures to illuminate problem areas and to focus an organization's attention. Decisions that result from all six core concept areas should be data-driven and aligned with the organization's strategies and targets.

Critical Issues and Future Trends in QMI

Integrating a QMI philosophy is not an easy process. Leaders in long-term care facilities need to be aware of several critical issues and trends as they embark on their quality journey. Like most industries initially implementing quality management, the health care industry is uncomfortable with the idea of collecting data for periods of time across entire processes. People tend to focus on individual occurrences and "fire fighting" in response to specific incidents rather than on researching long-term problems and patterns that are actually caused by the process itself. In health care the perception seems to be that collecting data across a whole facility ignores the needs of individual residents. However, time is well spent when it is focused on solving recurring problems in major processes, thereby helping every individual who is affected by that process.

Facing the barriers that are discussed in Chapters 4 and 5 also is an important early concern when implementing a continuous improvement process or refining an existing process. The first section of Chapter 5 addresses what may be the most fundamental issue in health care in the 21st century, status quo and the compliance mentality. Past regulatory practices have emphasized meeting standards rather than achieving breakthrough change. In addition, the traditional quality assurance mindset may limit the possibilities for quality improvement and cost containment.

Strategic planning flows from the six core concepts after they have been adopted by an organization as a fundamental belief system. The strategies managers develop will use QMI implementation guidelines and other QMI tools and techniques to address the barriers and other critical issues that arise; management's actions demonstrate their commitment to these changes in organizational culture.

Several critical issues that will dominate the health care industry of the future began to emerge in long-term care facilities in the 1990s. Managed care providers, such as health maintenance organizations, rely on quality management processes and principles to ensure that effective processes result in successful clinical outcomes. In addition to measuring clinical outcomes, long-term care providers must be able to measure the cost of care and service to negotiate contracts successfully. For example, the reimbursement strategy of capitation is based on average costs of health care per patient per month. Successful cost management depends on professional risk management that is based on accurate data and effective management systems. Using process measurement, outcomes data, and employee involvement in process control and improvement, the elements of quality management provide a strategy for effectively managing costs.

Compliance survey systems and reimbursement methods make the acceptance and implementation of QMI complex in most health care settings, particularly in the highly regulated long-term care environment. Electronic submission to state and federal agencies also makes reporting processes more complicated. QMI data collection and analysis tools often provide a consistent, easily understood process for documenting care given to residents of long-term care facilities.

The changing health care environment is complicated further by the numerous integrated delivery systems (IDSs) that are emerging in the form of networks, mergers, and other relationships among health care providers. As IDSs reduce the cost of hospital stays by substituting periods of rehabilitation at long-term care facilities, resident populations are becoming somewhat younger in age, with shorter average stays, and need higher-skilled postacute nursing care. These systems require quality management tools and data analysis to measure and evaluate customer needs and to select optimal long-term clinical outcomes and effective service delivery processes, all at a cost-effective rate.

Reaching for Excellence Through QMI

The goals of QMI in long-term care include the following:

- Improving customer satisfaction among all customer groups
- Maintaining a systems orientation, that is, an awareness of how related processes affect one another
- Openness to employee involvement, continuous process improvement, and process measurement concepts
- Providing optimal long-term clinical outcomes for residents
- Establishing a consistent, predictable, successful, and increasingly cost-effective process across groups of employees and residents
- Reducing the risk of fines or decertification
- Management systems that base decisions on facts/data

Measurable results include reductions in costs of quality and improvement in long-term competitive position due to increased customer satisfaction. Although these measurable results are sometimes difficult to quantify because they are "soft" figures, we provide several sets of possible metrics that may help managers track the outcomes of their quality management implementation efforts.

The 3-Phase Quality Management Integration Process

Although there are no recipes for implementing quality management, facility leaders (with the administrator at the helm) must plan strategically for the facility's transformation. The 3-phase quality management integration process (see next page and Appendix A) suggests a framework for a facility's planning efforts. This process may guide implementation in one department, in one facility, or across a multifacility organization. The 3-phase quality management integration process is explained in Chapter 3.

Applying QMI Principles and Processes: Woodland Care Center

The story of QMI at Woodland Care Center, a long-term care facility in a suburb of a large metropolitan city, demonstrates many of the critical issues that must be addressed in a QMI process. (Woodland Care Center is a pseudonym; however, the details of the case study are factual. Woodland's case is discussed in depth in Chapter 3 and is carried throughout the book.) This story describes the initial stages of QMI at Woodland Care Center and reflects the experience of other long-term care facilities. The various issues and pitfalls are typical of QMI implementation in widely varying organizational cultures. The causes of these problems are examined throughout the book, and we provide solutions and warnings for management for each issue explored. The QMI tools introduced provide continuous quality improvement, an unending search by staff and management for additional cost savings and customer satisfaction, with improved employee job satisfaction and reduced employee turnover as natural outcomes.

About Woodland Care Center

The facility described in this case study is part of a nationwide organization whose corporate quality function teaches and facilitates QMI throughout the organization. This

The 3-Phase Quality Management Integration Process

Phase 1—Priorities, Strategies, and Objectives
- Identify desired outcomes and goals for the QMI process
- Conduct preliminary needs assessment in departments and at local sites
  - Management roles
  - Employees' and supervisors' perceptions of quality
  - Current data: history of regulatory compliance, customer or employee satisfaction surveys, clinical data, and so forth
- Prioritize or modify goals

Phase 2—Implementing the Quality Improvement Process
- Communicate purposes of quality management process to organization
- Establish quality structure: quality council, management roles
- Conduct training in basic quality principles
  - Managers/supervisors, followed by employee groups
- Identify key management/supervisory processes and measurements
- Identify customer needs
- Determine critical success factors and establish a system to measure them
- Initiate projects selected by quality council

Phase 3—Continuous Improvement of the Quality Management Process
- Maintain momentum!
- Expand scope of participation throughout organization
- Establish clear accountability in management and employee groups for implementing QMI concepts in daily work life
- Monitor process and outcome measures to drive planning and decision making
- Ensure effective communication systems throughout the organization
- Refine and reassess success of QMI process continually
- Reexamine customer needs, concerns, and results at frequent, scheduled intervals

process was called TQM at Woodland. Training was first provided at a seminar offered to corporate staff and the administrators of all of the facilities in the organization. Woodland Care Center then engaged an external consultant to begin its quality planning and initial QMI integration.

An ongoing concern in health care is the translation of generic (commonly accepted) quality management concepts into the vocabulary and procedures of the specific organization. This ensures that employees understand the concepts and expedite their implementation. It is fortunate that the structure and vocabulary provided to Woodland Care Center by its national parent group were thoughtfully developed for health care. The guidelines and overview materials used to introduce the quality management system were compatible with other accepted TQM and CQI systems. The vocabulary, format, and approach were simply adapted to the long-term care environment. This translation of generic quality management vocabulary enabled Woodland's staff to understand the concepts quickly.

Initial planning for the project fell to the administrator, and the first overview and training sessions were offered to Woodland's department heads 6 weeks later. At the start of the project the facility's census included 113 Medical Assistance residents, 5 Medicare residents, 45 private pay residents, and 7 veterans, totaling 170 residents. The size of the staff was 190 employees, including 150 nursing staff. There are three resident floor units at Woodland:

- Floor 1 residents are higher functioning, more independent, and require less skilled nursing care than Floor 2 or 3 residents.
- Floor 2 residents display cognitive and behavioral impairment, such as dementia or Alzheimer's disease, and they require somewhat more skilled care than Floor 1 residents.
- Floor 3 residents require the most skilled nursing care for a variety of medical conditions, and they often display multiple medical problems. Increasingly, they may be temporary convalescents in need of subacute care after hospital stays.

In the first strategic planning session with Woodland's administrator, the 3-phase quality management integration process was initiated. The activities and processes of Woodland's QMI project illustrate how QMI principles and concepts enable process improvement and employee involvement. Each of these processes and activities is described in later sections of this book.

Evaluating Success at Woodland Care Center

When the key outcomes of Woodland's QMI project were evaluated, they included the following:

- Senior staff introduction and acceptance of QMI principles and methodology (with pre- and postevaluations)
- Establishment of process measurement, improvement, and evaluation at regular intervals, as opposed to data collection simply to satisfy regulatory agencies (quality improvement projects completed in each department)
- Clear definition of customer groups and acknowledgment of their needs (illustrated by family satisfaction surveys that are administered periodically by Woodland staff and Woodland's participation in the annual state-administered compliance survey process)

- Optimistic expectations by senior staff for further improvements in work processes and quality of work life (pre- and postevaluation QMI survey)

The evaluation and interpretation of these findings are discussed in later chapters.

Woodland's experiences illustrate the quality journey faced by many organizations in the initial phases of QMI. The outcome of the QMI project at Woodland Care Center was an expanding, well-accepted quality management process. Continued success depends on the leadership and communication efforts of Woodland's senior staff, particularly the administrator and the quality council.

Summary

The keys to success lie in incorporating the guidelines-for-excellence concepts in a facility's strategic planning for implementing QMI. As managers lead the transformation process, they should consider how they will integrate the core concepts of customer focus, continual learning, employee involvement, systems orientation, continuous process improvement, and leadership into their daily work life and plans. The examination of the six core concepts of the QMI model, along with the QMI implementation guidelines, have provided the "big picture." Successful QMI implementation rests on understanding the model and basing decisions on process and outcomes data. The 3-phase quality management integration process guides strategic planning for quality management success. These models and guides are developed further in later chapters and the appendixes.

References

1   Goldratt, E.M. (1990). *Theory of constraints.* Great Barrington, MA: North River Press.

2   Goldratt, E.M., & Cox, J. (1986). *The goal: A process of ongoing improvement.* Great Barrington, MA: North River Press.

Chapter 2

THE EVOLUTION OF QMI

HISTORY, TOOLS, AND TECHNIQUES

How did the concepts of continuous quality improvement (CQI) and total quality management (TQM) develop? Tracing their historical roots, this chapter highlights the evolution of the principles of TQM and CQI—in manufacturing, where they were born, and in service industries and health care delivery organizations. This chapter also includes two mini-cases that illustrate QMI implementation in health care.

Examining the Historical Roots of TQM and CQI

Ensuring high quality originally was the duty of the craftsmen or professionals who produced a product or service. In the early to mid–1900s, however, manufacturing companies began using the assembly line, and the quality function evolved to one of quality control and inspection. The quality of the end product was determined by an inspector or auditor. This quality control or quality assurance specialist was responsible for ensuring that the product that was delivered to the customer was free of defects. An adversarial relationship often existed among the inspectors and those being inspected. In addition, this method resulted in a great deal of waste, both in time and product, because when a defect was noted in the end product, it either had to go back for rework or was thrown out.

As organizations begin recognizing the problems with pure quality control methods, responsibility is returning to the individuals producing or providing the product or service. The resulting process may be called *quality improvement, organization-wide quality control, continuous quality improvement (CQI),* or *total quality management (TQM).* Thus, quality has traveled across time, with shifting definitions and with different individuals taking responsibility for achieving it.

The contributions of many quality practitioners and leaders are reflected in today's quality management practices. However, the work of W. Edwards Deming and Joseph M. Juran from the United States and Kaoru Ishikawa from Japan resulted in major changes and new ideas for implementing TQM.

It was after its defeat in World War II that Japan picked up the gauntlet and resolved to create a quality revolution that would win the so-called trade war. The Japanese invited Deming and Juran to give lectures on how to achieve this goal. The statistical methods were covered by Deming; Juran addressed the quality improvement methods.

Juran emphasized that crucial to achieving improvement in quality was the importance of management taking a leadership role. He insisted that every department from top to bottom become involved in TQM; this way, concerted action could be taken when problems arose. He also emphasized that there be a continual effort to improve on quality, not simply an annual effort.[1]

Juran's quality trilogy model (see Figure 2-1) has had a profound effect on many quality systems and many successful quality managers. The quality trilogy includes quality planning, quality control, and quality improvement.[2]

W. Edwards Deming and the Plan–Do–Study–Act Cycle

Whereas Juran particularly addressed improvement of management methods and quality planning ("most problems lie within the system"), Deming especially focused on involving all frontline employees in process improvement and on using data to analyze, stabilize, and improve work processes. One quality improvement tool that Deming developed for data analysis, the Plan–Do–Study–Act, or PDSA, cycle,[3] has had a profound impact on every industry—manufacturing, service, government, education, and health care.

The PDSA cycle is used to study the typical behavior and output of a process in order to gain "profound knowledge" of the causes for its variation. Deming previously had spoken of the cycle phases as plan–do–*check*–act. He changed *check* to *study* because he felt that *check* implied simple inspection rather than a long-term investigation of process behavior and a deep understanding of how to achieve process control and optimize performance. The PDSA cycle shown in Figure 2-2 provides details of the QMI activities in each phase of the model. This cycle also may be called *a continuous improvement process.* In the diagram the arrow provides the fifth cycle element by implying "continue to improve; do it all over again." The arrow stands for the continual improvement that refines work processes. Therefore, these processes stabilize at increasingly better performance levels through time. The continuous improvement element is a required component of both the model and the powerful improvement process that it represents.

Every process can be improved using the PDSA cycle. Use data to identify key process problems and assign a team to work on them. Focus first on the most significant processes and priorities. Examples of these processes and priorities in the long-term care industry

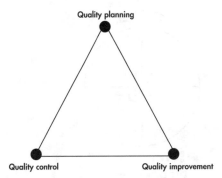

Figure 2-1.   Juran's quality trilogy.

range from admissions to discharge and from preplanning to final billing. Remember that using data to track key indicators helps focus the study at each stage of the PDSA cycle and warns managers if the process starts slipping to its previous levels of performance.

Implementing TQM and CQI in the Service Industries

TQM was introduced to the service industries in the 1980s. Bankers, retail operators, and restaurant managers began singing the "customer service anthem." Bookstore shelves filled with books on how to improve the quality of service. Phrases such as "the customer is always right," "the pursuit of excellence," and "you have only one chance to make a good first impression" became the rallying cry for service companies that recognized that lackluster customer service would leave them in the dust of their more successful competition.

Jan Carlzon from Scandinavian Airlines System (SAS) taught quality professionals and business managers the importance of managing the customer's experience. In 1981 Carlzon became the president of SAS, which at the time was operating at an $8 million loss. Through his unwavering commitment to service management, he was able to turn the company's loss into a gross profit of $71 million in little more than 1 year. It was Carlzon who introduced the concept of "moments of truth" and defined them as being any episode in which a customer comes in contact with any aspect of the company and thereby has an opportunity to form an impression. This meant that an organization had to create a work environment in which all employees were oriented to customers. Another side of SAS's success was Carlzon's basic philosophy of making sure that the company really is selling what the customer wants to buy. Customer groups were segmented so that their needs could be addressed.

During the same period, there was a growing understanding that there are two types of customers: internal and external (see Chapter 1). The *external customer* is defined as the purchaser of the product or service, and the *internal customer* is an employee within the organization who depends on another's work to provide what the external customer expects. For example, for the bank teller to meet the needs of his or her customer, the bank manager must provide the teller with the appropriate information and tools to permit a positive interaction with the external customer. The teller, in this respect, is an internal customer to the manager. Similarly, the teller is the internal customer of the human resources and payroll departments (see the exhibit on p. 23).

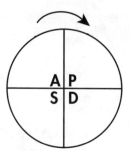

Plan
List processes
Identify a problem area
Get customer input

Do
Measure
Chart the data
Make a flowchart
Brainstorm changes
Select a change
Try it (field study)

Study (check)
Measure
Confirm improvement with customers

Act
Put change into effect permanently if
  results are good
Communicate changes
Set up intervals to monitor process

Continue to improve
Get customers' input
Monitor process at scheduled intervals to
  confirm improvement is maintained
Continue to improve or select another
  process

Figure 2-2.   The Plan–Do–Study–Act cycle, a continuous improvement process.

In addition to the change in perception of "the customer," there also was a heightened awareness of the importance of employee satisfaction. Businesses began to recognize that a strong correlation existed between the level of customer service and the degree to which employees were satisfied with their work environment. Increased emphasis began to be placed on understanding employee needs and motivations, recognizing that employees who were frustrated by factors such as unappreciative supervisors, unresponsive managers, or limited advancement opportunities would be hard-pressed to practice good customer service skills.

Although they were developed originally for process control and continuous improvement in manufacturing, quality management efforts support all industries. Health

Making Customer Service More than a Slogan

Once a quality management philosophy is adopted, a complete transformation of an organization's culture must take place. McLaurin and Bell[5] addressed the challenges that a change of this magnitude presents. With a quality management perspective, management must change its ways of thinking about and dealing with "customers": Who are customers? Management must come to accept the fact that each employee is not only part of the organization but also is a customer of the organization. Management's goal is to enhance the quality of care and service by improving customer service. These results depend on the workforce. Employees can make the difference between success and failure of the quality management process.

To ensure success, management must assume a leadership role in the changes that need to take place within the organization. They must provide support during implementation to achieve changes in employees' attitudes and behaviors. All levels of the organization, from senior management to frontline employees, must change their ways of thinking about customer service. Because communication is key to any successful implementation, managers tracking progress on a regular basis ensures that excellent customer service becomes a reality, not just a slogan.

care organizations, including long-term care facilities, have begun to incorporate these powerful concepts successfully into day-to-day operations.

Implementing TQM and CQI in the Health Care Industry

Quality practitioners can be found in all industries—nonprofit, for-profit, government, and education. Many health care organizations have discovered the value of quality management and have implemented QMI processes with great success. All of these industries are emphasizing customer needs and customer satisfaction as the driving forces behind the changes. Long-term care is no exception.

As the health care industry began to use quality management processes, the classic tools and techniques were adapted further, proof of their fundamental usefulness. However, as health care organizations adapted these concepts, several differences between manufacturing and health care became apparent. Mueller[4] discussed how TQM as practiced by manufacturing employees differs from TQM as practiced by health care personnel. He pointed out that health care providers are professionals and independent decision makers. Often, the nature of their work is highly stressful and does not lend itself to "by-the-book" TQM. In health care the customer usually is part of the process as opposed to being the end user of the process. This human factor makes health care processes more difficult to measure.

To be successful with their quality initiatives, health care executives first had to recognize that undergoing the quality management process required changing the way that they operated their business.[5] They had to face a number of issues that literally meant changing the way that they thought about the provision of care and services. These issues are data-driven decision making, understanding and anticipating process variation and seeking its causes, delineating the role of the health care manager in QMI implementation (see training and certification information in Chapter 7), implementing a customer focus in health care provision, overcoming a regulatory-compliance mindset, and understanding the differences between quality improvement and quality assurance.

Data-Driven Decision Making

The health care literature stresses the use of quality data for consistent decision making as part of a system rather than treating each health care decision as an isolated incident. In addition to using data to improve the health of an individual patient or resident, health care providers are required to recognize how aggregate data can be used to improve care delivery for an entire resident population. Traditionally, facilities have collected large amounts of data for quality assurance reports but do not use the data for QMI decision-making purposes. Data are useless to an organization unless they are analyzed and then used to drive decision making and action planning. The display below provides guidelines for turning data into information on the success of the facility's processes and systems. Health care, as in other industries, often has measured success in terms of the service provider's criteria for success rather than the resident's (customer's) needs. In a quality management environment customer needs and expectations drive improvement initiatives. Customer satisfaction alone, however, is not the only measure that health care facilities need to consider.

To truly measure quality in long-term care, facilities must create a balanced set of key indicators that measure all aspects of the organization. Thomas Stofac[6] sounded a cautionary note about the thrust toward customer satisfaction in health care. He stated that customer satisfaction should be tied to long-term clinical improvement or rehabilitation,

"Data" versus "Information"

Despite volumes of data, managers often are not aware of possible customer satisfaction improvements or process efficiencies that are available to their staff; they have "data" but not "information." QMI tools and techniques help individuals to manage process outputs and to track actual, real-time process levels and trends.

Collecting meaningful data and turning it into useful information is one of the most important skills of a manager. Decisions based on solid data can save huge amounts of time and can resolve problems permanently.

Although data collection is important, it is easy to become overwhelmed by useless data, especially when collection is done without a clear purpose. In addition, data that could be meaningful are often collected, but few individuals take the time to convert them into useful information. The difference between the two terms must be kept in mind:

> **Data**—Raw facts and figures that are collected as part of the normal functioning of the facility
>
> **Information**—Data that have been processed and analyzed, so that the results are directly useful to those involved in the operation and management of the facility

To evaluate a facility's data collection efforts, the collected data must be identified, and the following questions must be answered:

- Why are these data being collected?
- Are the data being turned into information or just being collected?
- How will the data help the facility to meet its customer needs? To improve care or service?
- Are there data that are not being collected that should be?
- Are more data than can be responded to being collected?

not simply to short-term feelings of satisfaction by the resident or family. Clinical aspects of care should be a key driver of process improvement rather than simply improved scores on customer survey forms. Stofac's list of suggested CQI areas and a simplified data collection process are reproduced in Appendix D. In addition, facilities need to identify measures that reflect their financial health, the work environment, and the effectiveness of various practices within distinct populations.

Understanding and Anticipating Process Variation and Seeking Its Causes

Underlying each of the six core concepts that make up the QMI model (see Chapter 1) is a foundation of data measurement and analysis. Variation always occurs in processes, but to optimize a process and make it more predictable, the causes of that variation must be identified. It also must be decided whether variation is built into the normal, everyday procedures or whether it is truly a unique occurrence. These are the differences between typical variation (common causes and the effects they have on a process) and out-of-the-ordinary, exceptional special causes of process variation. In the following excerpt, managers in the long-term care industry are reminded of these differences and how the response should reflect what is learned about process variation. The examples are long-term care's service delivery system and a facility's response to customer feedback from both residents and family members and concerned friends (FCFs). Note that the processes/systems that must be changed often are management's daily routines and habits.

> Interestingly, ongoing feedback to the nursing home administrators about the satisfaction of the residents and the FCFs[7] is usually absent. . . . Nursing home managers commonly practice a form of "management by exception" when it comes to the satisfaction of residents or FCFs. Special incident reports (e.g., reports of medication errors or resident accidents) help to identify "special cause" problems in the system, but do not assist managers in attaining continuous improvement of daily service or care. [When a specific cause for a major change in a process can be assigned, it is identified as a "special" or "assignable" cause.] Without some type of ongoing feedback from customers and regular analysis of the feedback to provide a context in which to position the special cause problems, such problems may become an alternate source of priorities, further distracting managers from daily care issues.
>
> For administrators to improve daily service and have the ability to manage their own priorities, they need ongoing information that can identify common cause problems or problems that are caused by the current service delivery system. They can use such information to begin to reduce the variation in the delivery system. . . .
>
> Deming[8] . . . suggests that troubles and potential for improvement exist. Typically, 94% of organizational problems can be attributed to the system (common causes) and the remaining 6% are a result of special causes. Therefore, nursing home administrators are receiving and reacting to information that could make only a small difference in the current system.[7]

At Woodland Care Center, the senior staff reflect this common, well-intentioned, but largely ineffective emphasis on special causes and "fire fighting," rather than daily repetitive (systematic) common causes. Woodland's administrator frequently challenges these assumptions. When the QMI process is mature, quality council members also will provide leadership in ongoing process measurement and decisions based on data. Data analysis is fundamental to quality management, yet it is overlooked by most well-intentioned problem-solving managers. They are unaware that reacting to special causes ("management by exception") without modifying the underlying system of common causes may increase, not decrease, variation and inconsistency in their processes. (Regulatory agencies usually reflect a similar bias, which is examined in Chapter 5.)

Health Care Manager's Role in QMI Implementation

The manager's role in supporting a change in culture and in developing a continuous improvement process is key to any quality management implementation. Management sometimes tries to delegate the change effort elsewhere in the organization, thereby avoiding improvement of its own management processes. This action only weakens the implementation process and signals lack of involvement to the organization.

Juran emphasized the importance of management's leadership role in any quality effort:*

> *Many upper managers concluded that quality is the responsibility of the quality department. This belief made it easier for departments such as production [including health care service production] to give top priority to other parameters.*
>
> *Upper managers became detached from the quality function. Many concluded that by delegating quality to the quality manager, they could devote their own time to other matters. As they did so, they became progressively less informed about quality. Then when the crisis came, they lacked the knowledge needed to choose a proper course of action.[9]*

This focus on management's role is not intended to de-emphasize the fact that, regardless of the quality systems that are adopted, it is the direct care and service providers who must deliver excellent care and service. These frontline service providers can contribute recommendations for change based on their daily experience with residents and families and the organization's established service delivery processes. In the long-term care environment, employees are frontline decision makers every day in every customer interaction. Management's contribution is to establish the systems and provide the training, monitoring, and flexibility that allow frontline care providers to meet customers' (residents') needs with a minimal number of barriers.

Customer Focus in Health Care

The behavior of employees who are direct care and services providers profoundly affects both resident and family customers. An understanding of who the customer is and how to

---

*This excerpt was part of Juran's series of speaking engagements in 1993–1994, "The Last Word: Lessons of a Lifetime in Managing for Quality." He explained to management their leadership roles in the total quality management effort. Additional excerpts are found in Appendix B. The barrier to quality management success that is caused by management's "detachment from the quality function" is examined in Chapter 4.

relate to customers is a fundamental skill that is required of all employees, but especially of those who interact directly with residents and families. Smith[10] directs attention to two distinct aspects of customer service:

> *The service, once provided, cannot be inspected or recalled. The customer's perception of quality is as much influenced by the behavior of the service provider as it is by the results of the service process. Thus, both aspects of service must be the focus of an improvement effort.*

It is important to recognize that customer service in geriatric health care can be complicated further by attitudes of ageism, residents' learned helplessness, and other barriers to effective long-term clinical outcomes. (Measuring customer satisfaction of the important family/caregiver customer group is discussed in Chapter 6 and illustrated by the Family Satisfaction Survey in Appendix F. Administering the survey and statistical analysis of survey data are addressed in Chapter 6 and Appendix D.)

Regulatory Compliance Mindset

The long-term care industry is one of the most highly regulated industries in the United States. Nursing facilities are regulated much more than are acute care hospitals. Because of these regulations it is not surprising that residents sometimes find themselves secondary in importance to government compliance and regulatory agencies, despite the good intentions of managers, caregivers, legislators, and regulatory bodies.

As long-term care facilities have become more formal and regulated, an increasing share of their effort has focused on simply meeting regulatory standards. Implementing QMI is the most effective means of meeting resident needs while ensuring that the requirements of regulations, enforcement, and effective professional management are satisfied. This issue is examined in Chapter 5 as the *compliance mentality*. In a quality management environment enforcing compliance issues should be communicated to customers and employees alike as compliance with *minimal* standards, always subject to further continuous quality improvement, not as projections of ideal quality outcomes.

> *Bureaucratic governmental processes now determine quality care. What is lost is that these are minimum standards of care, rather than appropriate targets. This is the major barrier to a transition to Quality Management principles and continuous quality improvement, even above financial considerations. Consequently, these bureaucratic processes replace customer focus as the central core of Quality Management.*
>
> *Thomas Stofac, 1993*

Differences Between Quality Assurance and Quality Improvement

An important aspect of training employees in quality management is to contrast the traditional quality assurance model with the CQI model. Both models address quality, but one suggests audit and control mechanisms to "assure" quality and take corrective action after a problem has been identified (traditional quality assurance model), and the other suggests methods to "improve" quality on an ongoing basis (CQI model). Contrasts should be drawn between the inspection/detection and the planning/prevention paradigms. (See Table 2-1 for a comparison of quality assurance and quality improvement.)

The active leadership involvement and proactive problem solving done by employees that are necessary in QMI are quite different from the reactive problem solving done by senior managers. Although ongoing monitoring and auditing of processes is necessary, the data collected must be used to identify opportunities to enhance care and service and to make decisions on improvement priorities. The gradual shift by accreditation agencies from quality assurance to supporting quality management is significant. It is reflected both in setting regulatory standards and in assessing facilities and health care processes. The shift has not been fully implemented in standards for quality audits or assessor training, however, as detailed in Chapter 5, which has led to inconsistent survey processes.

Examining QMI Implementation and Results: Two Mini-Cases

Two success stories illustrate QMI implementation in health care. The first occurred at a large teaching hospital, the second in a long-term care organization. Look for many of the core concepts of QMI and elements of the 3-phase quality management integration process.

George Washington University Medical Center

Health care QMI that resulted in major cost savings and employee successes is embodied by George Washington University Medical Center (GWUMC). GWUMC is a large teaching hospital in Washington, D.C. The outcomes achieved by implementing QMI included effective teamwork and identification of potential significant savings in administrative areas, with resulting reductions in costs of quality and with measured improvements in customer satisfaction. Although this case illustrates QMI in a hospital setting, the cost savings experienced are comparable in many ways to the savings that are experienced in a multifacility long-term care organization. The processes that the staff addressed also are similar. Note the active leadership roles played by senior executives and the reflections of other core concepts in the QMI model.

Reluctance to use manufacturing quality jargon and other issues of TQM implementation, discussed previously in implementing TQM in health care, were reflected in a project at GWUMC. Although W. Edwards Deming was a faculty member at that time, GWUMC chose not to link its quality improvement process with Deming or with the industrial successes that were achieved in Japan. In April 1993,

> GWUMC administrators quickly realized that the transformation would require a major commitment from senior management. They also realized that the management team would be greatly challenged in translating the organization's philosophy into a clear vision of what a quality transformation would require.[11]

First, GWUMC's senior managers established a quality council headed by the executive officer and executive dean of GWUMC. Membership included research and academic affairs deans, the chief operating officer, the hospital administrator, the chief financial officer, the director of nursing, and the hospital medical director. Council responsibilities included the following activities:

- Formulating the quality policy that stated its mission, vision, and guiding principles
- Prioritizing opportunities for organizational improvement

Table 2-1. Quality assurance versus quality improvement

Topic	Quality assurance	Quality management integration
Motivation	Regulations/licensure	Enhance the satisfaction of internal and external customers Excel; compete effectively
Focus	Meet standards, solve problems	Prevent problems; improve continuously
Attitude	Required; defensive	Chosen; proactive
Target for improvement	Clinical; technical	Clinical; technical; customer satisfaction; employee retention
Type of model	Medical model	Process model
Who defines quality?	Health department	Customers
Who is responsible for quality?	Managers	All staff
Who evaluates quality?	State and federal governments	Organization, based on customer input and key indicators
Data collection	Department data tracking	Data collection and analysis by those closest to process, often interdepartmental teams
Scope	Selected departments; within functions	Organization-wide; within and across functions

- Supervising and supporting intradepartmental and cross-functional quality action teams as they move through their improvement journey
- Making a commitment to provide time for process improvement by employee teams
- Developing strategies for analyzing customers' needs and expectations

Second, the management team selected an experienced physician and former quality vice president from a leading health maintenance organization to be an external mentor/advisor, and they chose a well-respected senior assistant administrator for operating departments to be full-time coach, architect, cheerleader, and internal consultant. Training investments were significant: The entire senior management team was trained first; then the director of nursing, the administrator, and the medical director all served as faculty for a 20-hour introductory course for all managers.

Substantial cost savings were identified after approximately 3 years: GWUMC eliminated 300 staff positions and improved its bottom line by $10 million. (Like many organizations, GWUMC had "naively" anticipated early short-term, large-scale results.) It also was reported that teams implemented many diverse quality improvement projects. For example, during a 5-month period, the patient accounting department applied quality tools and techniques to reduce accounts receivable aging by 20 days, an 8-year low. Linens expenditures were reduced by $75,000 annually through another team's efforts. In response to patient surveys the obstetrics division of nursing improved patients' perceptions of care. Written complaints to the hospital decreased over a 2-year period, and the average waiting time in preadmissions surgical-screening processing decreased from several hours to 50 minutes.[11]

Summary

It must be emphasized that the quality improvement environment for long-term care facilities is different from that in hospitals, and it differs from state to state in financial reimbursement for provided services. The types of process improvements and cost savings described at GWUMC also are being considered at nursing facilities like Woodland Care Center and in multifacility long-term care organizations like Southwest Regional, a composite of the stories of several organizations.

Southwest Regional Health Systems

The quality management journey of Southwest Regional Health Services, a 14-facility long-term care organization, began with key management staff's realization that traditional quality assurance methods do not ensure quality. Southwest Regional had regulatory survey activity in two facilities that concluded with less-than-favorable results. Recognizing that resident quality of care and overall quality of life required a much deeper understanding and commitment from all levels of the organization, the organization decided to explore the concept of quality management.

Key staff members took it upon themselves to learn as much as they could about the philosophy of quality management and the implications of integrating such a philosophy into a long-term care organization. They discovered that, although there were many organizations in a variety of industries that had successfully implemented quality management, there was little documentation of success stories specific to long-term care organizations. These staff members looked closely at what acute care providers were doing and found varying degrees of success among hospitals. Through their research, it became very clear that management's commitment to this philosophy was absolutely essential to an organization's success in integrating quality management.

With approval and encouragement from the Southwest Regional Systems board, they retained an external consultant who had expertise in health care quality management. With assistance from the consultant and a quality management steering committee, a pilot training program was developed and implemented in 3 of the 14 facilities. At the end of this pilot program the decision was made to hire an internal consultant who could facilitate the integration of quality management throughout the organization. The management team then developed a 2-year plan for the integration of quality management. Its goal at the end of 2 years was to establish a quality infrastructure and other systems that would support quality management over a long period of time. (The quality infrastructure is the support structure needed to promote and support Southwest Regional's new organizational climate. Quality councils that include senior staff members and executive leadership teams are examples of pieces of the necessary decision-making structure.) The team felt that 2 years was reasonable to establish the foundation but recognized that full integration of quality management was a lengthier process.

The strategic plan included establishing a quality council within each of the facilities to serve as the forum that would guide that facility's management of quality. Southwest Regional also established an organization-wide quality council that defined the organization's quality management philosophy, policy, and standards. This corporate council defined the organizational systems that required strengthening to support quality management implementation. These key systems included data collection and analysis, performance management, staff development, and process management.

The quality councils identified key indicators that they continuously monitored for unacceptable variation. If they noted special cause variation, then they explored the cause; if they noted unsatisfactory common cause variation, then they chartered a process improvement team to study the process and make recommendations for improvement.

Process improvement teams began working on prioritized areas, and efficiencies and cost savings such as the following were discovered in many aspects of care and service processes:

- One process improvement team studied the accounts receivable process and reduced its aging by 50%.
- Another team studied the admissions process and was able to streamline admissions by enhancing interdepartmental communication and improving the efficient flow of paperwork.
- Measurements of resident and family satisfaction improved as a result of these changes.

Summary

Southwest Regional Health Systems is fairly new at quality management, but the organization already has experienced some of the benefits that result from strong leadership and effective strategic planning. Although the organization continues to struggle with both internal and external barriers, the management team has tasted success and is anxious to continue learning and move forward with the integration of quality management in its day-to-day operations. In many ways the team models the benefits of implementing the six core concepts of QMI and data-driven quality management in daily work life. In addition, the integration of quality management has flowed more smoothly by applying the 3-phase quality management integration process.

Summary

This chapter has traced the historical journey of the principles of TQM and CQI, from their beginnings in the manufacturing industries to the application of these generic tools in service industries such as banking. As these powerful tools and techniques moved into health care, they took on health care terminology and implementation requirements. The tools are generic, and this book provides implementation guidelines and long-term care–based applications. The term QMI emphasizes their application to the six core concepts of the QMI model, which are founded on data.

The PDSA cycle, with its necessary "continue to improve" step, illustrates the process improvement side of QMI. The quality journeys of two organizations rounded out the chapter, using health care and long-term care QMI to illustrate the steps of the QMI quality journey.

As long-term care facilities seek to achieve improvements in psychosocial and clinical outcomes, in addition to cost savings, they will face other critical issues and barriers to QMI. Chapters 4 and 5 describe these further.

References

1   Juran, J.M. (1994, August). The upcoming century of quality. *Quality Progress,* 31–36.
2   This diagram is the authors' "artist's conception" of the Juran quality trilogy.
3   The seeds of the PDSA cycle concept originated with Deming's teacher and mentor, Walter Shewhart.
4   Mueller, R.A. (1992, April). Implementing TQM in health care requires adaptation and innovation. *Quality Progress,* 57–59.

5   McLaurin, D.L., & Bell, S. (1993, November). Making customer service more than just a slogan. *Quality Progress,* 35–39.

6   Stofac, T.J. (1994). Personal interviews.

7   Kleinsorge, I.K., & Koenig, H.F. (1991, December). The silent customer: Measuring customer satisfaction in nursing homes. *Journal of Health Care Marketing, 11*(4), 3. The authors discuss the need for continuous process improvement and ongoing communications of customer feedback from the residents and surrogate decision makers in nursing facilities. They call these surrogates *FCFs*—family members, appointed custodians, or concerned friends.

8   Deming, W.E. (1986). *Out of the crisis* (2nd ed., p. 315). Cambridge, MA: MIT Press.

9   Juran, J.M. (1994, August). The upcoming century of quality. *Quality Progress,* 30.

10 Smith, A.K. (1993, June). Total quality management in the public sector. I. *Quality Progress,* 45–48.

11 Chaufournier, R.L., & St. Andre, C. (1993, April). Total quality management in an academic health center, *Quality Progress,* 63–65.

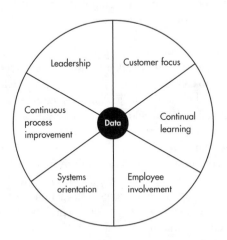

Chapter 3

IMPLEMENTING QMI
IN THE NURSING FACILITY

How does a facility ensure successful introduction of QMI concepts? This chapter opens with a "before-and-after" success story and then applies the six core concepts of the QMI model to a variety of settings. The chapter also highlights the many activities that took place during the early phases of the QMI process at Woodland Care Center as they illustrate the early implementation of the 3-phase QMI process. Note the emphasis on data analysis to set priorities and measure the success of process improvements. Displays spotlight other facilities' project activities and provide industry data that deepen readers' knowledge of QMI implementation requirements in the rapidly changing long-term care industry.

Carver Health Care Center Implements QMI

Carver Health Care Center began implementing a quality management initiative in the mid-1990s. The changes that have occurred during this time have brought a completely different feel to the facility than was the case prior to implementation.

Jim Barnes, the facility's administrator prior to implementing QMI, managed the facility using an autocratic leadership style. His sole focus was the bottom line. Department head meetings revolved around discussions of census and budget. When a department manager was over budget during a given month, Barnes immediately would call the manager into his office and rake him or her over the coals.

Barnes's approach to problem solving was to tell his department managers to "fix the problem, and fix it fast!" In an effort to respond, managers would apply short-term solutions and not take time to find the cause of the problem. Consequently, the same problems would come back to haunt the facility over and over.

Barnes's leadership style set the tone in the facility. Because he promoted competition between departments, department managers reflected a similar leadership style. Fear was the primary motivator for Carver's staff. Employees were reprimanded when things went wrong, and very rarely was recognition given for a job done well. The results were predictable: high employee turnover, low customer satisfaction, and decreasing census.

In 1996 a new administrator, Ken Parker, came on board. The atmosphere in the facility was influenced immediately by Parker's participative leadership style. He started by working with the staff to create a shared vision of where they wanted to take the facility in the next 5 years. He helped people to clarify the current status of the facility and then develop a plan of action that would move them toward their vision.

Parker recognized that a healthy bottom line would come as the result of paying attention to delivering high-quality care and service in an efficient manner. He established systems that would ensure that staff stayed in tune with customer needs and expectations. Surveys, focus groups, industry data, and family and resident councils provided information that developed into customer satisfaction improvement projects.

Parker also began encouraging a different kind of problem solving, one that focused on process improvement and that incorporated the Plan–Do–Study–Act cycle (PDSA; see Chapter 2) of continuous improvement. Although this methodology was new to the staff, they readily agreed to try it because Parker made it very clear that they had "to stop blaming each other and focus on improving the process." Solving problems became everyone's business as process improvement initiatives included employees who actually worked within the process being improved. Department head meetings reviewed QMI projects as well as old agenda items of census and budget.

Parker worked to break down barriers between departments by promoting a spirit of teamwork among department heads. He spent time building trust by establishing effective communication systems and supporting supervisors in developing participative management skills. The results were predictable: enhanced employee morale; improved customer service; and increased resident and family satisfaction, with a corresponding increased census.

Foundation of QMI: Knowing Who Is the Customer

As in many long-term care facilities, the management staff at Woodland Care Center recognized the need to increase their ability to respond effectively and efficiently to change while remaining responsive to their customers. It was this recognition that influenced their administrator's decision to explore the potential of QMI. By following Woodland through its quality journey, one can learn from its positive experiences as well as become aware of some of the barriers to avoid. During approximately a 10-week period, Woodland Care Center, with guidance from an external consultant, initiated a project that helped staff understand the philosophy, process, and value of QMI. The planned outcome of this project was to guide and facilitate the initial implementation within the facility. The timing of this proposal was fortunate because Woodland's national corporate group was beginning to implement several pilot QMI projects at sister facilities. The national organization offered QMI overview training in which Woodland's administrator was introduced to the concepts.

The cultural transformation of an organization undergoing a shift to QMI usually requires several years. (Some of the leaders in the field speak of 5–7 years, some even 10 years, before old management habits disappear fully.) The process begins with organizational leaders taking a firm stand on gaining a customer focus. To successfully integrate a quality management philosophy, facilities must be very clear about who their customers are and what motivates these customers. Like other long-term care facilities, Woodland's external customer base included four major groups: residents; family members, designated caregivers, or concerned friends; regulatory agencies; and payer groups. Although other constituencies, such as physicians and hospital discharge planners, are sometimes called customers, these four groups generally are considered to be the primary external customer groups.

Residents of long-term care facilities, unlike the customers of other industries, may have little or no say about which facility is selected because frequently these decisions are made by family members or designated caregivers or by payer sources such as health maintenance organizations. Although assessing needs and satisfaction levels of residents is essential, it is also important to assess the needs and satisfaction levels of the other three customer groups. This feedback provides significant information to facility staff. Examples of customer needs assessment data and surveys of the friends and caregivers group are examined in Chapter 6 and Appendix F. Compliance surveys of Woodland by the regulatory agencies that govern a facility's certification also are discussed in Chapter 6.

Resident Profile at Woodland Care Center

The residents at Woodland are divided into three floor units that provide different levels of care:

> Third-floor residents receive skilled nursing care for a variety of medical conditions, and they often display multiple medical problems. Residents may receive subacute care following a hospital stay, convalescing for their move back to their homes. Residents of other floors also may temporarily need higher-level care. As managed care organizations increase their use of long-term care facilities for short-term, postacute care, Woodland's staff are caring for a changing demographic base in this unit: Residents are younger, with a markedly shorter length of stay, and are in need of sophisticated and technologically advanced care.
>
> Second-floor residents typically have cognitive or behavioral impairments, may have Alzheimer's disease or other forms of dementia, and require moderate levels of nursing care.
>
> First-floor residents are the most independent and capable residents. They require the least amount of nursing care.

Changing Demographics in Long-Term Care Facilities

Woodland resident statistics reflect the rapid changes that are found in all long-term care populations, their needs, and their expectations. As a result the professional care providers who serve them need flexible processes that enable accurate, timely decisions, often using incomplete information. For example, shorter-term resident stays require discharge planning that begins on the first day of the stay; thus, the admissions process, a critical system in any facility, requires frequent attention. As the proportion of shorter-term residents increases, facilities compete for longer-term, more stable residents. Therefore, quality of care and customer satisfaction are key elements in process–improvement efforts. For many facilities process improvement efforts have focused on the admission and discharge of residents and have resulted in significant streamlining of these processes for staff as well as enhanced customer satisfaction of residents and families.

Changes in Woodland's third-floor subacute residents increased rapidly during a span of 3 years, causing changes in the overall population statistics of the facility. This 2-year snapshot of Woodland's statistics reflects ongoing changes statewide and in the long-term care industry as a whole. The implications for Woodland's strategic planning and nursing-care processes are apparent:

Year 1:   44% of new admissions had length of stay in facility of less than 42 days (6 weeks)
          Average length of stay for new admissions—21 days
Year 2:   50% of new admissions had length of stay in facility of less than 42 days (13.6% increase in 1 year)
          Average length of stay in Year 2 was 18.6 days (11.4% reduction)
          Average length of stay for new admissions—19% had less than 1-week stay
          50% of discharges were to home or to assisted living facilities
          30% of discharges were due to death (related to higher acuity/severity of illness in third-floor unit and to availability of hospice care for terminally ill residents on all three floors)

Implementation of QMI Project Plans: 3-Phase Quality Management Integration Process

As a facility applies the six core concepts of QMI and the 3-phase quality management integration process (see p. 15 and Appendix A), the results are higher customer satisfaction ratings, increased operational effectiveness, and cost reductions. Each facility's implementation will vary, depending on the local organizational culture, but many activities are common to most QMI implementation processes.

Successful QMI advocacy requires a solid understanding of quality management and an unwavering commitment to quality management principles from the leaders in the facility. The 3-phase quality management integration process is designed to provide leaders with a framework for a successful integration of quality management principles, resulting in customer and employee satisfaction and process effectiveness.

Phase 1 is primarily a planning stage in which desired outcomes and goals for the quality process are established. Strategic quality planning begins early in this phase. An assessment of the facility's current status also should provide an awareness of management's and staff's current understanding of QMI concepts. Phase 2 of the implementation integrates a variety of QMI activities into the organization's daily routine and involves more managers and staff in process improvements. Most of the Phase 2 QMI activities carry into Phase 3 as momentum is maintained and a new organizational culture and new management habits are established. This culture change requires several years.

This chapter provides examples of the ways in which Woodland Care Center addressed the QMI activities by phase, so that QMI process implementation can run in a timely, smooth manner. (Remember that every facility's culture and openness to change is different. Thus, the details of Woodland's QMI implementation differed somewhat from Carver's and other mini-cases that are found in this book, but most QMI implementation procedures are very similar in content and purpose.)

Early planning meetings with Woodland's administrator established the intent to focus efforts on the 15 management staff members who would be charged with leading the entire staff's QMI process, which they called TQM. Department heads who reported to the administrator included the director of nursing, dietary director, social services director, occupational therapist, recreational therapist, physical therapist, speech-language pathologist, medical records director, housekeeping and laundry director, maintenance director, and business office director. Three nursing supervisors also were included in training and quality improvement projects.

For a variety of reasons Woodland had been headed by four different administrators in 2 years, so it was particularly important that its QMI process be stable, widely accepted by staff members, and successful (i.e., demonstrate worthwhile results). The administrator was particularly concerned that department managers be knowledgeable about continuous quality improvement (CQI) techniques and expected outcomes so that they could support the implementation. To that end QMI project selection and training initially were limited to the department managers. Activities that involved the entire staff were planned to take place when the initial quality management introduction had been completed with department heads, after managers became more comfortable with their leadership role. The nursing staff, headed by the director of nursing, would be central in importance at that time. Of 190 staff members, 150 provided nursing care for Woodland's 175 residents.

The consultant and administrator planned the following implementation activities during Phases 1 and 2 of the 3-phase quality management integration process:

- Conduct preliminary needs assessment and identify goals for the project.
- Conduct a quality management survey (pre- and postevaluations of senior staff attitudes).
- Establish a quality council.
- Define a "road map" for the quality journey (e.g., Baldrige Quality Award guidelines—see p. 42—or other QMI implementation process).
- Conduct QMI overview and training.
- Implement department-level quality improvement projects.
- Establish a communications team.
- Establish interdepartmental communication/collaboration systems.
- Establish interfacility communication systems (specific to multifacility organizations).

Phase 1: Priorities, Strategies, and Objectives

Identify desired outcomes and goals for the 3-phase quality management integration process

Conduct preliminary needs assessment in departments and at local sites
  Management roles
  Employee and supervisory perceptions of quality
  Current data, including history of regulatory compliance, employee or customer satisfaction surveys, and clinical data
Prioritize or modify goals

Preliminary Needs Assessment Tool

Phase 1 is a time to gain an understanding of senior management's degree of knowledge and acceptance of quality management principles. A series of needs assessment interviews may be conducted to determine the current level of understanding and commitment that exists in the top managers related to quality management. The interview structure is found in Appendix I.

Phase 1 begins by identifying desired quality results anticipated for the organization and defining specific process goals. Thus, outcomes are measurable against a standard, noting trends through time. The QMI leadership team or quality council then develops strategies to move toward these goals. The goals provide an outline of intended outcomes for each step of the quality journey. Plans include ways to cascade the goals down into daily work in all organization departments and processes.

At Woodland, Phase 1 consisted of discussion and an agreement between the administrator and the external consultant on strategies and goals for the integration project. A second meeting included the individual to whom the role of quality improvement coordinator was assigned. After discussion on how to proceed, the consultant was introduced at the department head meeting, and goals and training plans were outlined briefly for the department head and nursing supervisor group.

Quality Management Survey (Pre- and Postevaluations)

The only way to determine how a facility really knows whether progress is being made with QMI efforts is through measurement. A frequently used method is to define a baseline measure, perform the same measure later, and then compare results. A survey of senior staff attitudes toward quality was used in this way at Woodland. Fourteen members of the management staff at Woodland completed quality management surveys as pre- and postevaluations to quantify and rank their perceptions of the facility's quality overall. They also identified specific issues and concerns to be addressed during the QMI implementation project. The following issues received the most consensus in the preevaluation and were identified as important topics for problem solving and project selection:

- Need for improved communications, including interdepartmental communications
- Difficulty of providing adequate time for QMI activities
- Reluctance to change
- Need for a positive attitude
- Need for strong, broad-based management support for quality

The same survey was completed by the management staff as a postevaluation after approximately 10 weeks. There was a 19% improvement in overall quality in management assessment of quality between pre- and postevaluation scores. The staff attitude survey and the survey results are contained in Appendix E; Chapter 6 describes the uses of survey data.

Managing with data is at the heart of effective quality management. During Phase 1 an inventory of current measures is evaluated to establish baseline data. These measures include the results of compliance surveys and clinical, financial, and human resources data. Data that provide insights into customer expectations and satisfaction are also reviewed.

Examples of customer data include resident and family council input, customer complaints, and satisfaction surveys.

Phase 1 assessment, goals, and outcomes vary somewhat among long-term care facilities, depending on local and organizational circumstances. However, Phase 1 always provides preliminary strategic quality planning and actively involves the administrator and senior staff in QMI implementation. One organization's preliminary strategic quality planning document is reproduced in Appendix G. This document outlines many of the considerations to be addressed by the senior management leadership team and the quality council. These types of documents can be adapted to fit any organization's culture and level of quality sophistication.

Phase 2: Implementation of the Quality Improvement Process

Communicate purposes of QMI process to organization
Establish quality structure: quality council, management's roles
Conduct training in basic quality principles
   Managers/supervisors, followed by employee groups
Identify key management/supervisory processes and measurements
Identify customer needs
Determine critical success factors and establish a system to measure them
Initiate projects selected by quality council

In Phase 2 of the 3-phase quality management integration process an organization's management staff implements the plans that were developed during Phase 1. To translate to the language of the Malcolm Baldrige National Quality Award, the "approaches" that were developed in Phase 1 are "deployed" in the processes and projects of Phase 2. As the quality management process becomes more familiar to senior leadership, it spreads wider and deeper among employees at all levels of the organization. As decisions are based increasingly on process data, one should gradually detect improvement in "results" or outcomes data. (Using state and national Quality Award criteria to improve performance excellence is described in more detail later in the chapter.)

Leadership and Strategy: Role of the Quality Council

To sustain a change effort of this magnitude, an infrastructure must be established that consistently supports quality improvement efforts. This leadership group may be called the continuous improvement council, the quality leadership team, or another name, but the importance of the quality council's leadership role (see display on p. 40) cannot be overestimated, especially in the early months of a change in culture. (The QMI process is "owned" by facility staff, not by the quality consultant.) In addition to process improvement teams that work on specific projects, there are ongoing department teams, often called natural work groups, that address their own process issues and improve customer satisfaction. Figure 3-1 illustrates a sample infrastructure in a multifacility organization.

The quality council will find two tools to be of great help as it assesses the needs of the facility and its own leadership role in the quality management effort. The QMI model, with its six core concepts and its reliance on data for making decisions, ensures that all aspects of quality management are considered when discussing the possible courses of action.

(For a review of the implementation guidelines that accompany each concept, see Chapter 1.) The 3-phase quality management integration process ensures the quality council's long-term focus when discussing issues such as problem solving, project selection, or resource allocation. The Sample Quality Management Plan (see Appendix L) also is help-

Leadership Roles in QMI

Administrator
Commitment of the senior manager (e.g., administrator, CEO, president) is vital to the success of QMI. He or she provides leadership for the transition to a QMI environment and resources to develop the infrastructure for implementing the quality management plan.
- ✓ Provides overall leadership to the quality management initiative
- ✓ Chairs the quality council meetings and other planning meetings
- ✓ Leads a strategic planning process that results in actionable key business drivers
- ✓ Holds employees and managers accountable for QMI
- ✓ Uses data and information in decision making
- ✓ Supports continuing education in QMI
- ✓ Models and supports the development of QMI attitudes and skills

Department Managers
Members of the management team must actively model the organization's quality management philosophy and champion quality improvement activities. Quality leadership cannot be delegated if initial QMI momentum is to be maintained.
- ✓ Practice, teach, and model the principles of quality management in words and behavior.
- ✓ Give process improvement team members the time to attend team meetings and perform team responsibilities.
- ✓ Provide staff with data, information, and resources.
- ✓ Establish communication channels for staff to share quality improvement ideas.
- ✓ Stay informed concerning the status of quality improvement efforts.
- ✓ Support staff in implementing solutions, and recognize them for their accomplishments.

Quality Council
The quality council's role is to provide direction and communication on quality issues for facility managers and staff. To this end, Woodland's quality council had oversight responsibility for the following areas:
- ✓ Performs strategic quality planning for the organization
- ✓ Addresses customer requirements and satisfaction issues
- ✓ Provides guidance and oversight of QMI process
- ✓ Identifies and prioritizes improvement needs
- ✓ Coordinates organization-wide QMI activities with the corporate office
- ✓ Assesses and identifies training needs
- ✓ Communicates QMI principles throughout facility
- ✓ Monitors organizational outcomes
- ✓ Allocates resources, including financial, staff, and information
- ✓ Selects key processes and measurable indicators to align organization's QMI efforts at every level

ful in the quality council's Phase 2 deliberations. Appendix K contains guidelines on the quality council's roles in guiding QMI implementation. In this appendix, Caldwell discusses both "accelerators" to QMI, which many senior leaders know, and "inhibitors," which often are overlooked.

For the most part, quality council membership includes management or supervisory staff and people who actively guide the QMI process. Therefore, managers must clearly understand their role in implementing these strategies. (Occasionally, employee team leaders may rotate membership, particularly in mature programs or self-directed teams.) The administrator and department heads set the tone and create the pace for QMI implementation in all departments. The leadership roles checklist guides senior leaders' roles in QMI implementation. The key to success is to create an infrastructure that is not separate from the care operations of the facility. Quality planning, quality control, and quality improvement should become "the way to do business." As a result, instead of creating a separate quality council, some organizations simply reshape their routine management team meetings with a format that includes strategy and planning, outcomes analysis, and project management.

Woodland's first quality council was composed of the administrator and four department managers: the directors of nursing, medical records, social services, and housekeeping/laundry. The administrator selected the members with the anticipation that these roles would

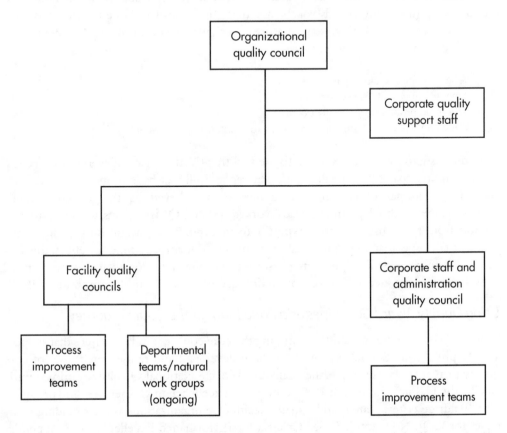

Figure 3-1.   Sample infrastructure of an organizational quality council in a multifacility organization.

rotate among department heads. Active participation by both the administrator and director of nursing was crucial and nondelegable, however. (Further discussion of the quality council's role is found in Chapter 4.)

Applying Training and Measurement to Improve Process Performance

Providing consistent and ongoing employee training and orientation addresses the need to systematically reduce and control variation in resident care delivery processes. Reducing process variation helps to ensure consistent, stable resident care. When staff are trained and held accountable for using best practices, care outcomes are improved and predictable.

Monitoring both processes and outcomes permits the identification of unwanted process variation and the improvement of processes before they reach a crisis point (i.e., risk management). Unless outcomes are monitored and measured over time, variation is often misunderstood. When managers do not understand variation, they place blame or give credit to people for things over which the people have no control. One of the senior managers on Woodland's quality council said, "We all already know where the problems are." Clearly, this manager did not recognize the wide variations in understanding QMI principles that exist among department heads and the even wider variations among staff employees. Furthermore, this manager tended toward fighting recurring problems rather than preventing them by changing the process.

Woodland Care Center's administrator felt that questions to address in QMI included the following (in quality awards vocabulary, these questions would be translated as "systematic approaches," "deployment," "process design and continual improvement," and "prevention" of recurring problems):

> What systems are already in place?
> Are we following those systems?
> Where do problems frequently occur?
> What can we do to change the processes so problems do not recur?

The administrator frequently stressed to the staff that QMI is a part of everyday processes, not an activity separate from daily work. She recognized that basic problem-solving skills are an important part of teaching QMI concepts. She believed that the greatest momentum was gained as the department heads worked on their QMI projects, with one-to-one support from the consultant (the "expert"), to incorporate applications of quality management concepts that were previously introduced in formal training. In effect, this on-the-job training added to previous classroom learning. The consultant recommended reassessment of the success of classroom training, perhaps at 3- and 6-month intervals.

Using Quality Award Guidelines as a Road Map for the Quality Journey

Structural considerations include identifying the core concepts and principles that support a QMI philosophy. Several organizations have developed and refined such a set of core quality principles. For example, the Malcolm Baldrige National Quality Award was initiated by the U.S. government in 1987 to promote excellence in U.S. services and products. The "Baldrige criteria" are used by many health care organizations as their guiding principles for CQI. Now entitled the "Criteria for Performance Excellence" (see Appendix

C), the Baldrige framework is promoted as a structure for self-assessment rather than primarily as an application for the Quality Award. Beginning with the 1999 award cycle, any health care organization (for-profit or not-for-profit) may compete within its own industry, using health care vocabulary and concepts. Appendix J provides details about ordering free single copies of the Criteria for Performance Excellence.

The seven "categories" in the new health care criteria are

1. Leadership
2. Strategic Planning
3. Focus on Residents, Other Customers, and Markets
4. Information and Analysis
5. Staff Focus
6. Process Management
7. Organizational Performance Results

Attached to each of these seven facets of quality are criteria that address the characteristics of high-performing organizations. For example, in the Staff Focus section, there are specific items related to hiring and retention practices, training practices, and human resources planning practices. Woodland's quality council studied the Quality Award guidelines established by its state, which were modeled on the Baldrige criteria, and used the seven categories as a road map for its quality journey. Appendix C provides examples of applying a Quality Award road map to an organization's quality journey and illustrates how the quality council's QMI leadership activities demonstrate all seven aspects of the Baldrige criteria. To see improved results in their process and customer outcomes, the quality council and other quality leaders must both plan systematic approaches to improve quality and follow through and deploy those plans throughout the organization.

Woodland's quality council members decided to rotate the seven categories; council members in other organizations frequently become champions of just one category. All seven areas need leadership and oversight on an ongoing basis, regardless of how category oversight is structured. The priorities addressed by the quality council included interdepartmental coordination, resource allocation, communications and recognition issues, and promotion of data collection and analysis.

QMI Overview and Training for Senior Leaders

Woodland's administrator, department heads, and the three nursing unit supervisors (a total of 15 senior staff members) attended initial QMI overview and training with the consultant. The training objectives for that session were as follows:

- Develop a shared definition of quality.
- Discuss the characteristics of quality leadership, and begin to practice them during the session.
- Survey the tools and techniques of quality improvement and process management that make up QMI.

- Plan how to initiate application of QMI concepts to Woodland Care Center and to staff jobs.

Woodland's parent organization already had developed mission and vision statements. The following philosophy/principles of QMI, as outlined by the parent organization, included many foundation concepts of quality management:

- Satisfying customers
- Managing with data
- Preventing errors
- Leading and empowering
- Improving continuously

The attendees at the QMI overview session brainstormed a broad range of definitions of quality. Woodland's 15 senior managers identified the following desired outcomes of QMI:

- Provide services in a caring environment to all of the residents of this facility in order to maintain or improve an individual's functioning at his or her highest level with dignity.
- Provide/maintain a good quality of life for residents.
- Quality should be defined by a customer's needs and requirements.
- Employ quality practices in marketing against the competition.
- Use progressive ideas to compete successfully.
- Maintain the highest standards of care.
- Set a goal of zero complaints from residents.
- Offer a variety of services.
- Maintain high standards of building upkeep.
- Be well staffed with high-quality personnel.
- Find a solution to every problem—no excuses!
- Maintain good hiring practices (leads to professional service and attitudes).
- Encourage good teamwork.
- Make it clear that staff are important.
- Be aware of the costs of problems in quality.

Creating this list of definitions broadened the perspectives of the individuals who received the training. Participants were able to move beyond the compliance mentality in which quality merely means meeting established process standards. This comprehensive understanding of quality dovetailed nicely with the parent organization's definition of quality: "Meeting or exceeding customer expectations at a cost that represents value to them." This definition is not based on theoretical excellence of product/service or on corporate priorities; thus, clearly, it is both customer based and realistic.

Acceptance of QMI concepts depends in large measure on communicating a "win-win" scenario for department heads and other professional staff. QMI training should illustrate personal stress and costs caused by current systems and should incorporate success stories from other organizations to demonstrate the benefits of CQI. The fundamental purpose of QMI, however, should be to address long-term gains for residents, with a secondary interest in other customer groups or internal customers.

Department-Level Quality Improvement Projects

With a structure in place, priorities defined, and initial QMI overview training completed, Woodland Care Center's quality council continued Phase 2 of the 3-phase quality management integration process. Each department manager chose a specific intradepartmental project to which he or she could begin applying the concepts of quality improvement. The managers detailed the project outcomes to the administrator and provided brief updates at department manager meetings. Many projects were selected by or included nonsupervisory department staff, although the quality improvement projects were not to be introduced as QMI projects in the departments until after the formal staff introduction to QMI principles; at first, they were simply improving the way that staff work. In an effort to provide a successful first project for the department heads the administrator asked each department head to choose a fairly straightforward, short-term project. Woodland's summary report on quality improvement projects and results is reproduced in Table 3-1.

Staff and managers accept QMI principles more readily if they grasp their usefulness, so that QMI is not "just another program" or a fad. Understanding the six core concepts of the QMI model through overviews and training helps both management (first) and staff (thereafter) in implementing the QMI tools and techniques effectively. Management's commitment and accountability become apparent in whether the staff accept QMI core concepts as part of their daily work. Management by fact relies on the application of the six core concepts, each with a foundation in data analysis. QMI should be communicated, both in training and in daily practice, as the way that the organization's vision is implemented and organization priorities are set.

The administrator and department head together identified these projects as improvement targets, but Woodland's administrator stressed that staff should integrate quality management principles and tools in their daily functions. QMI was not to be considered as separate from their job responsibilities but as the way that they carried out their responsibilities every day. Overall, the experience was very well received, and the department heads clearly were pleased with the results and the reception that they received from other staff members. A number of department heads requested that another set of projects be initiated immediately.

The overview training session included a good discussion of the management by fact concept. Despite preliminary planning meetings with both the consultant and the administrator, only 5 of the 15 projects actually collected and analyzed data. Most projects were simple, straightforward, and in need of little quantitative justification. During the overview, however, there had been a discussion of the PDSA cycle of continuous improvement as emphasized by Deming and the management by fact concept. For future projects, Woodland has an opportunity to apply the PDSA cycle of continuous improvement to its QMI process in order to refine its effectiveness of QMI and project selection. The administrator needs to encourage staff to include measurable variables and at least some simple, formal data analysis as they approach their next project. Thus, these staff leaders and their department teams have an additional chance to experience success in a controlled environment and truly practice quality improvement techniques using management by fact.

One decision to consider in each process is whether an individual or an informal group, rather than a formal QMI team, should address problem areas. The display on page 47 illustrates factors to consider in the decision "to team or not to team."

Table 3-1.　Quality improvement projects in the departments

Department	Project	Outcomes
Administration	Decrease telephone paging (noise) and increase receptionists' efficiency	Reduced noise in corridors
Staff Development	Develop new safety checklists for unscheduled audits; results reported to Quality Assurance & Safety Committee	Each department list complete, scheduled by month
Therapeutic Recreation	Reactivate newsletter committee for families; recruit volunteers and residents; include reader survey with future issue	Folding and preparation time reduced for staff and committee[a] Communications ensured with residents' families
Housekeeping	Reduce clutter in stairwells, "garbage"	Discussed with staff
Laundry	Label residents' clothing	Effort ongoing
Occupational Therapy	Reduce morning interruptions	Requested, later thanked staff for improvement[a]
Nutritional Services and Speech Therapy (joint)	Improve quality and appearance of thickened liquids; decrease time spent in preparation	Good response; survey developed for staff/resident reactions[a]
Maintenance	Monitor temperature of warm water in residents' rooms	All within appropriate and safe range of temperatures
Social Services	Revise several forms for resident communication, admissions processes	Better communication with residents, more effective computer entry of data
Business Office	Track time sheets and errors in paychecks; causes of handwritten checks	Reduced clerical time, "rework" time; staff to punch in correctly
Nursing	Projects chosen by floor's staff	All projects monitored for continued improvement; employees pleased with results
First Floor	Organize residents' personal items so they are accessible; reduce clutter	Staff finds items more quickly and in consistent location Complies with infection control practices
Second Floor	Similar project for a more dependent and vulnerable resident group	Similar successful result
Third Floor	Nursing assistants establish "buddy system" and revise break schedule to ensure coverage on floor	Improved coverage; to be monitored
Medical Records	Manual developed for each floor's audit requirements	To be distributed and monitored

[a]*Indicates that quality improvement project incorporated data collection and analysis before making a decision on solution (5 of 15 projects).*

To Team or Not to Team

Criteria to consider when using teams

Identify the project precisely; define the problem clearly

Collect data and information that enable effective decision making

Build consensus around the solution to the problem—among management, among staff members, or between groups; ensures employee or management "buy-in"

Encourage employee self-sufficiency; accustom managers to let go of decision making in carefully selected projects

Include knowledgeable stakeholders from all parts of the process; often, managers know general steps and outcomes but are not aware of detailed procedures and, especially, rework and preprocess setup details

Gather data on a problem; research; benchmark other organizations' best practices (including those outside the industry)

Remove the worst inefficiencies or achieve the largest savings; focus on rework, waste and scrapped materials, and preprocess setup (e.g., paperwork, computer, supplies, transportation of people or materials); delays between steps and hand-offs among units and departments

Provide opportunities for enthusiastic involvement and excitement at the appropriate level for each individual (e.g., managers and clerks are bothered by different types of problems); provide resources that are adequate for project success, including preliminary training and/or team facilitation

Sources for projects

Begin with vision/mission and annual operations plan

Projects with survey or regulatory implications

Client risk

Client or family needs

Management needs

Cost of problem

Projects identified by employees as high priority

Notes on team management

Consider the first project to be a learning experience for the team; initially, the group may seem less than productive.

Begin with a project that likely will be successful within predetermined time limits. Be sure that the team understands expectations and time limits or other parameters of the project.

If you establish an employee team/task force, then be prepared to accept and implement its recommendations. Or, you may wish to request the team's research or insight but clearly reserve decision making for management (e.g., the holiday work-scheduling issue requires major policy changes, but teams can research the costs entailed, the impact on the community, and so forth).

When employee recommendations cannot be accepted or will be only partially implemented, explain the causes to the employees as fully as possible.

Develop and use a robust, consistent problem-solving process for team activities, such as the PDSA cycle. This ensures effective use of the team's time and improves the likelihood of the success of the project.

Interdisciplinary Quality Improvement Project

The quality council identified the short-term stay unit on Woodland's third floor as having several improvement opportunities, including specific nursing care issues, timely documentation, and the rehabilitation therapy process. Because these issues involved multiple disciplines, the process improvement efforts were interdepartmental. This quality improvement project was very challenging because it involved a cross-functional team, but it is one that would greatly benefit Woodland's customers, specifically the residents on that floor and their families. The council believed that this quality improvement effort also would improve Woodland's relationships with the physician groups and health management organizations that call on Woodland's short-term stay unit with increasing frequency.

Communicating QMI Efforts

A communications team was established to communicate QMI efforts to Woodland staff. The team planned several informational and fun events that introduced employees to this new way of thinking and working, and it began to create a long-term plan for ongoing communication. Woodland's managers recognized the need to establish good communications throughout the facility. One brainstorming activity that took place during the initial QMI overview was to list communication vehicles that were available to Woodland's management staff and the communications team. The available means of communication included the following:

> Department head meetings, staff meetings (leave some staff on duty), department meetings (divide larger departments), one-to-one meetings, staff "celebrations" such as a party following successful completion of annual survey
>
> Routing memoranda (to and from), other written memoranda, copies of good professional articles to stimulate discussion
>
> Department mailboxes, payroll check enclosures, "gifts" such as memo pads to serve as memory joggers for staff
>
> On-the-job training, in-service training
>
> Bulletin boards, notices posted by time clocks and on walls and doors of rest rooms/locker rooms or stairwell doors, announcements on public address system (minimized to control noise level)
>
> Facility newsletter to residents, family, volunteers
>
> Corporate/multifacility: e-mail, conference calls, multifacility quality meetings

Expanding the scope of participation throughout the facility required the use of these existing means of communication as well as others.

In response to staff requests for vital information, a previously used communications effort, the morning meeting, was reinstated by Woodland's administrator. The morning meeting had been an opportunity for staff to learn which department heads were in the facility each day and to share information such as admissions, discharges, meetings, and in-service training sessions. The meeting had been eliminated because it had become too lengthy, and, consequently, many staff did not attend. After it was discontinued, however, staff found that they missed the daily updates. The meeting was rescheduled as a "stand-up" 5-minute-long meeting in the administrator's office. The application of continuous improvement made the meeting time effective. Appropriate communications efforts are so central to effective QMI that they must be reassessed frequently by quality council members, the administration, and the dedicated team.

Interdepartmental Communications/Collaboration

The need for better interdepartment support and communications at Woodland elicited responses from 12 of 14 respondents on the preevaluation QMI survey. Addressing this need became a priority at Woodland. Several joint efforts served to enhance interdepartment communications. For example: 1) the staff development, nursing, and speech-language pathology departments developed new in-service offerings, including resident care planning process and drug interactions; and 2) Medical Records developed manuals for each unit on the different procedures and reimbursements among HMO payer groups. Woodland's administrator planned to share these manuals with sister facilities, thus extending the communications and process improvement issues among facilities. Several department managers specifically stated that they had noted improvement in their own and others' communications and willingness to collaborate since the QMI project began.

The communications team at Woodland was charged with communicating about QMI, although it is important to note that overall direction and policy originate with the administrator and the quality council. During times of stress or organizational change, two-way communications are vital to maintaining excellence in resident care and staff focus. The responsibility of leadership to communicate clearly, openly, effectively, and in a timely manner cannot be exaggerated.

Management Commitment Keeps Process Moving

After the initial 10-week period in which QMI was introduced at Woodland, the expansion of QMI training and communications throughout Woodland's nonsupervisory staff was targeted as the next key integration step. This step was pursued informally because the administrator wanted to ensure middle management's understanding of and commitment to QMI principles and goals.

The reality of implementing QMI is that even the best-laid plans can be sidetracked temporarily; therefore, planning must include flexibility. For example, the communications team's initial plans included a staff QMI kickoff for the whole facility, but the kickoff was postponed because of a week-long state compliance survey and its follow-up time commitments for corrective action. (One powerful incentive for continued process improvement could be the state survey team's follow-up survey.) A pizza party held later celebrated the successful results of the annual survey.

Phase 3: Continuous Improvement of the Quality Management Process

Maintain momentum

Expand scope of participation throughout organization

Establish clear accountability in management and employee groups for implementing QMI concepts in daily work life

Ensure effective communication systems throughout the organization

Monitor process and outcomes measures to drive planning and decision making

Refine and reassess success of QMI process continually

Reexamine customer needs, concerns, and results at frequent, scheduled intervals

The discussion of Phase 3 activities focuses mostly on what is expected of a maturing quality management process, what group processes and functions can be anticipated as QMI progresses, and how the organization can maintain the initial excitement about and momentum of the QMI processes. "Holding the gains" from previous improvement planning and deployment is a phrase used often in Phase 3. The senior leadership role continues to promote, support, and recognize quality improvements and manager/employee involvement. Deming would call this a "constancy of purpose."

Maintaining the momentum of quality management requires strong leadership and change management skills. Transforming an organizational culture takes time, effort, and persistence, even in the face of adversity. The following are some specific ways to maintain momentum:

- Consider whether all six core concepts of the QMI model are reflected in decision making.
- Incorporate data collection and analysis as a routine part of the decision-making process.
- Work to create an environment of trust between managers and staff, between departments, and between shifts.
- Monitor process and outcome measures to drive planning and decision making.
- Develop conflict management and negotiation skills.
- Make continuous learning an expectation of every job.
- Keep employees informed of facility goals and progress toward the goals.
- Find numerous ways to communicate successes.
- Practice the PDSA cycle in all projects and process improvement efforts, including tracking key process indicators at regular intervals.
- Make it easy for people to identify and communicate opportunities for improvement.
- Remain focused on customer needs and expectations—listen to what customers are saying.
- Continue to monitor key processes on a regularly scheduled basis so that upcoming shifts or trends can be anticipated.

An essential part of maintaining quality management momentum is the ongoing training and education of staff. Rather than approaching the process of ongoing training in a haphazard manner, it is best to target specific training needs by conducting a training needs assessment. A tool that can be used by the quality council to assess (and periodically reassess) QMI training needs (see display on p. 51) addresses the current level of knowledge and skill in the organization in a number of areas and enables senior leaders to rank their priorities to focus resource expenditures. Using this tool also achieves consensus among members of the council who may otherwise have very different needs and priorities regarding training.

As QMI projects wind down, their success should be assessed, both for their application of QMI principles and for their effect on process effectiveness and on process outcomes/results. This reflection process helps to refine the organization's application of QMI concepts. Examples of reflective thinking include the following questions:

- Were quality improvement projects selected from the highest-priority problems?
- Did individuals and teams use time well and minimize conflict?
- Were results communicated well and was recognition provided?
- Do the data show that the process improvements were worthy of the effort?

Assessing QMI Training Needs

Complete this assessment individually; then compile quality council scores, and reach consensus among quality council members.

Indicate the current level of knowledge that you feel your organization has attained in each of the following areas. In the "Priority" column consider the need for further training and indicate the priority levels of each knowledge/skill area for your organization. Rank each area as 1 (low) through 5 (high).

Name _____

	Competencies					Priority
	Limited (very limited knowledge/ skill)	**Adequate** (enough knowledge to apply personally)		**Proficient** (able to facilitate and teach/coach others)		**Priority** (significance of competence to organization)
Cultural change						
Organizational culture	1	2	3	4	5	
Leadership roles in integrating quality management	1	2	3	4	5	
Managing and accepting change	1	2	3	4	5	
Building commitment	1	2	3	4	5	
Managing resistance to change	1	2	3	4	5	
Systems thinking						
Organization as a system	1	2	3	4	5	
Work as a process	1	2	3	4	5	
Customer–supplier relationships	1	2	3	4	5	
Quality council						
3-phase quality management integration plan	1	2	3	4	5	
Quality management philosophy and standards	1	2	3	4	5	
Identification and assessment of customer needs	1	2	3	4	5	
Quality council communication plan	1	2	3	4	5	
Chartering process improvement teams	1	2	3	4	5	
Record keeping (e.g., tracking key process indicators)	1	2	3	4	5	
PDSA cycle	1	2	3	4	5	
QMI tools						
Operational definitions	1	2	3	4	5	
Stratification (subgrouping) of data	1	2	3	4	5	
Flowcharts	1	2	3	4	5	
Cause/effect diagrams	1	2	3	4	5	
Run charts	1	2	3	4	5	
Pareto diagram	1	2	3	4	5	

(continued)

	Competencies			
	Limited (very limited knowledge/ skill)	**Adequate** (enough knowledge to apply personally)	**Proficient** (able to facilitate and teach/coach others)	**Priority** (significance of competence to organization)
Team and meeting management				
Meeting process skills	1　2	3	4	5
Ground rules	1　2	3	4	5
Roles of members	1　2	3	4	5
Group dynamics	1　2	3	4	5
Idea-generating tools	1　2	3	4	5
Meeting records	1　2	3	4	5
Knowledge of and access to professional development resources				
Books, journals, and other printed materials	1　2	3	4	5
Community speakers and resources for QMI development	1　2	3	4	5
Membership in professional organizations	1　2	3	4	5

QMI Support in the Multifacility Organization

In a multifacility, national organization, such as the company of which Woodland is a part, QMI ideas can be communicated and shared among facilities. For example, Woodland's department managers shared ideas regarding computer formats for record keeping and resident intake with their counterparts in sister facilities. The national organization also organized a forum to support the sharing of best practices among and between facilities. The organization's need for in-house QMI support and organization-wide consistency in quality and service led to the hiring of its national director of quality management, who also serves as a liaison to promote organizational learning and sharing.

Summary

As illustrated by the Woodland and Carver case examples, the following factors are common in successful continuous improvement processes:

- Initiate strategic quality planning at the outset.
- Establish quality infrastructure such as a quality council or quality leadership team.
- Maintain senior management involvement.
- Provide training.
- Begin quality improvement projects so that departments or teams feel that they "own" the changes.
- Reassess progress continually (continuous quality improvement).
- Always make decisions based on collected data.

Much of this chapter has highlighted various activities that occur during effective implementation of the 3-phase quality management integration process. As demonstrated by Woodland, the culture of any facility will affect, to some extent, the types of quality improvement activities that are undertaken. Specific activities that occurred during Woodland's start-up project included the following:

- Overviews and training for department heads and the quality council addressed leadership and management skills, as well as tools and techniques for continuous process improvement.
- Baldrige Quality Award guidelines provided a framework for the quality council to assess success in a broad range of QMI activities. Other quality road maps may provide QMI direction.
- Use of pre- and/or postevaluation results from the QMI survey provided focus for department head activities during meetings and formal training sessions.
- Key management and supervisory processes were identified, and process measurement was begun.
- Quality improvement projects ensured "ownership" of their department processes by senior staff and employees during QMI activities.
- Communications efforts and interdepartmental collaborations supported involvement by the senior staff and employees.

Changes in demographics, medical technology, and the corporate environment affect skills needed by frontline care providers. Frequent reassessment of training needs by the quality council and the administrator are needed to maintain momentum in the quality management process, improve excellence of care, and reduce staff friction and anxiety in response to the rapidly changing health care environment. All selected QMI activities and projects should result in one or more of the following measurable outcomes: Long-term clinical outcomes for residents are optimized, costs of quality are reduced, competitive position of the facility is improved, employee satisfaction in delivering health care services is increased, and customer satisfaction with the facility is enhanced.

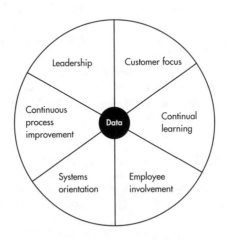

Chapter 4

INTERNAL CRITICAL ISSUES

To assist you in implementing quality management integration (QMI), consider several critical issues and potential barriers that can affect your efforts. This chapter investigates these issues and barriers to QMI that are internal to long-term care facilities and corporate chains; Chapter 5 examines the issues and barriers that are external to facilities or outside corporate walls, factors in the health care industry, and the political environment. The pointers in these chapters help administrators, quality professionals, and staff anticipate problems and smooth out the rough spots in the quality journey. The pointers are related to many of the six core concepts of the QMI model and to their reliance on data-based management by fact.

Illustrations from Woodland Care Center's quality journey are included, as well as how QMI can be integrated in a long-term care setting, how quality professionals can gain support from physicians, and how a good-quality data collection and analysis system can simplify the transition to QMI.

A variety of factors may limit the acceptance of QMI principles by employee and management groups. It is wise to begin the quality journey with a full understanding of potential pitfalls. In addition to reviewing Chapters 4 and 5, readers may want to network with quality management professionals and other health care professionals who are knowledgeable in the practice of process improvement, employee involvement, the use of data to measure process changes, and other quality management topics. Many of the critical issues and barriers faced by Woodland Care Center and other long-term care facilities are reviewed in the growing body of professional literature that covers total quality management (TQM) and long-term care.

Woodland Presents Common Barriers and Critical Issues

Many issues and barriers to the acceptance and implementation of QMI concepts and processes existed at Woodland and often looked similar to those encountered at other facilities or in the professional literature. Some of these issues and barriers and the actions that should be performed by senior staff were identified by Woodland's 15 senior staff members in pre- and postevaluations. The preliminary data collection survey and its results are found in Appendix E. Results of this QMI survey provided direction and areas of focus for Woodland's QMI process, especially for discussions of strategic quality planning with Woodland's quality council and administrator. A preliminary needs assessment such as this is an important part of Phase 1 of the 3-phase quality management integration process.

QMI Factors Unique to Health Care

For the most part, quality improvement projects in long-term care follow common patterns of implementation in the service and manufacturing industries. Woodland's process, however, illustrated some differences that are specific to health care industries, as compared with other service industries or manufacturing.

Translation of Generic TQM/CQI Vocabulary and Concepts to the Health Care Environment

The senior staff at Woodland Care Center were better able to translate the classical manufacturing vocabulary and concepts of TQM to their workplace than were many other service and industrial groups. Their flexibility may be attributed in part to their administrator's focus on improving resident care, a growing knowledge and acceptance of continuous quality improvement (CQI) in society in general, and their genuine desire to deliver excellent care to their customers. Another enabling factor is rooted in the values and ethical issues that are fundamental to any health care process: Health care itself is already a process of "continuous improvement" of services, clinical outcomes, and customer/family satisfaction. Care providers are organically and biologically trained, and they are not hindered by the industrial paradigm of a perfect, unchanging mechanical process. Health care employees anticipate ideal performance or complete process stability in their outcomes to a lesser extent than employees do in manufacturing. After all, people are never unchanging, so their health care processes should not be expected to be perfect and unchanging.

Medical apprentices and students have been instructed in techniques to change (i.e., improve) the patient's (customer's) health status. To a great extent, process improvement is a concept that already is found among professional employees in health care facilities such as Woodland Care Center. Public debates arise when health care providers become too focused on the needs of payer groups and regulatory agencies without considering the needs of patients/residents and families who are their primary customers. Although continuous process change is associated with rehabilitation and nursing care in the long-term care environment, two closely related concepts of QMI frequently are absent:

- Measuring and studying aggregate, or collected, data on overall systems and processes and basing decisions on that analysis rather than simply responding to individual patients as seems best at any specific time (QMI practitioners must learn how to apply common cause analysis rather than respond to special causes, as discussed in Chapter 2.)
- Basing decisions on long-term customer satisfaction with optimal clinical outcomes rather than simply seeking short-term resident happiness or satisfying regulatory standards (Regulatory standards should be a *floor*, not a *ceiling*.)

Long-Term Care Providers Are Not Factory Workers!

In health care industry processes, as in all service industry interactions, the frontline service provider is part of the process as much as is the customer. Decisions made by frontline health care providers are truly independent, professional decisions that not only affect people's lives and safety (as in other services such as the airline industry) but also may cause long-term physical or psychosocial changes in their customers, the residents themselves. Examples are the use of physical restraints, which may result in the loss of independence of residents, or the tone of voice and expectations for resident behavior that are communicated, often unknowingly, by frontline care providers. The role of a care provider in a long-term care facility is to be fully involved with and active in the delivery and ongoing improvement of the process of resident care. Unlike the relatively stable mechanical processes in manufacturing, health care providers must make decisions daily that ultimately alter residents' clinical outcomes. (By contrast, in a typical manufacturing approach to process improvement, the provider of the product is an outside observer of the work process who acts on the process.)

Other genuine differences from classical quality management issues in manufacturing are discussed in Chapter 2 and include the following:

- The rapidity and extent of changes in resident demographics are caused by changes in managed care organizations, networks among care providers, and other market factors.
- Setting process goals requires a flexible approach to future change and continuous improvement. Because people are never fully consistent or predictable, strategic planning must anticipate change and provide flexibility. Again, health care is an organic, not a fixed, process.
- The shifting balance between the needs of customer groups is particularly unlike other industries. All organizations address the satisfaction of customer needs, but the long-term care residents who are the primary customers often do not make their own health care decisions or decide to purchase the health care services provided. Other customer groups such as families, payer groups, and regulatory agencies usually make determinations for residents.

These challenges and many others face care providers and supervisors daily when they arrive at work. The only constant that they should anticipate is that change is always present.

Internal Organizational Barriers

Every organization that intends to implement QMI faces challenges from existing organizational culture, management practices and policies, and other internal barriers within the walls of the facility itself. Thus, each facility's QMI process will differ. Drawing from our experience with QMI implementation in long-term care facilities, we have developed the following set of 13 barriers that should be addressed early in the QMI process. Each barrier is discussed in terms of long-term care. We also provide commentary on Woodland's experience as it relates to each potential barrier. These potential barriers to QMI are avoidable with careful planning and consideration. Discussion of each barrier includes one or more possible interventions to offset it. Many other routes are open to an organization. These include the six sets of implementation guidelines associated with the QMI model and the 3-phase quality management integration process, which provides a framework for successful process improvement and solving problems.

Inconsistent Support and Commitment from Top Management

The chief misunderstandings found in all industries, including long-term care, are "we already know where the problems are" and "we have always used these process improvement techniques." It is a difficult transition from concentrating on caring for the individual resident and tracking his or her individual outcome to taking a systems–orientation approach by recognizing that care delivery is a series of interrelated processes that can be improved. Taking a systems approach means seeking methods to analyze "common cause" factors that determine process behavior and outcomes. It is the role of top managers to spearhead this new way of thinking and to demonstrate this belief through their actions. We cannot stress enough the overwhelming importance of top managers' support and involvement to the success of establishing a QMI focus. To reiterate Dr. Joseph Juran's statement, "Leadership is a nondelegable role."

Woodland was fortunate to employ an administrator who provided vision, a methodical approach to learning about QMI and its benefits, and strong leadership for the senior staff, yet did not dominate the process in a proprietary way. Members of the quality council differed in their acceptance of QMI principles and benefitted from guidance by the administrator and one another's progressive understanding of their leadership roles. On Woodland's initial quality management survey, 14 senior staff respondents gave the highest score in response to the question regarding management support for quality (on average, a rating of 7.16 out of a possible 10). Thus, commitment from top management (the administrator) was not perceived to be a problem at Woodland, yet the department heads differed among themselves in their understanding of and commitment to QMI.

To avoid this first barrier, facility leaders must demonstrate, through their words and actions, their commitment to quality. A facility's quality progress must be at the top of every meeting agenda. The administrator must define clear expectations for department managers and hold them accountable for those expectations. Participating in QMI cannot be an option for managers. Support and communication efforts should not waver.

There is no alternative to addressing the organization's needs for leadership. Senior management's active leadership role drives the culture change required for QMI and facilitates changes among both middle management and employees. Leadership cannot be delegated lower in the organization, as Juran emphasized.

Short-Term Focus

Short-term and "fire fighting" activities usually are reactive responses that result in temporary solutions to problems. QMI is a proactive approach that continually engages people in studying and improving processes. QMI calls for a long-term focus, and this type of approach results in more effective and longer-lasting solutions. Costs are reduced, employees display greater job satisfaction, and, most significant, residents and other customer groups are more satisfied with the care provided.

At Woodland the primary long-term focus seemed to be a general acknowledgment that processes can and should be more effective and should flow more smoothly. As in most health care settings, there is an expectation of continuous improvement of each resident's outcomes. Methodical, systematic process measurement and goal setting is the next phase of quality council proceedings and department head attention. Some facilities find this shift to long-term focus, via management by fact, to be a major hurdle.

An action that tends to exacerbate a short-term focus is the practice of examining point-in-time data. For example, if the infection control committee looks at only this quarter's infection rate, then it has no data with which to compare this rate. Conclusions and decisions are made without clearly understanding what this infection rate means in the context of previous data (the common cause system). To avoid this barrier, the data should be analyzed over time. Changes in levels of performance, trends, and variability or fluctuations in performance should be observed over time. The cause-and-effect relationship between things should be anticipated. When a management action is considered, managers should take the time to think through not only the short-term results but also the long-term implications. Measurement intervals for key indicators should be chosen based on how quickly the process can get out of control (e.g., ask whether the process needs to be tracked hourly, weekly, or monthly or whether a quarterly interval is sufficient for understanding process behavior).

Lack of Vision and Strategic Planning

Top managers should envision what quality can mean to the organization, embodying their vision in the long-term strategic quality plan. Creating a vision of the desired future begins by asking "What do we want our facility to look/feel like?" and "What kinds of relationships do we want to have with our customers, employees, and community?" The best way to create the desired future is to develop a clear picture of what management wants that future to look like and then develop a plan to create it. Including all of the employees in envisioning the future enhances the power of this process.

It is essential that a facility's vision and strategic plan be prioritized and communicated from top management to all department heads, who then cascade the plans into their departmental actions and employee communications. Although developing a compelling vision and strategic plan can be challenging, deploying the plan is even more challenging. From the strategic plan, specific outcome measures must be identified that will help facility management monitor its progress. The level of progress should be tracked and posted so that all staff members understand and can become aligned with common goals. (Thus, strategic approaches are deployed and lead to improved results and process outcomes.)

Strategic planning should include all six core concepts of QMI and the data being tracked in each. The organization uses the QMI implementation guidelines (see Chapter 1) and other QMI tools and techniques (e.g., 3-phase quality management integration process, PDSA cycle) to identify projects and issues that deserve top priority in planning and deployment. Organization leaders and quality council members act as role models as changes in corporate culture take place. Individuals doing the initial planning should acknowledge that early process changes may take place, followed by employees and managers gradually slipping back into old habits and attitudes.

At Woodland frequent one-to-one discussions between department heads and the administrator communicated the vision of future benefits for both staff and residents as well as other customers. Quality improvement projects also were discussed in terms of this vision.

Incomplete Knowledge or Understanding of QMI Principles

Knowledge may be taken to mean *applied training*, that is, implementation of concepts and techniques learned in training sessions. *Understanding* may be as broad as the vision mentioned previously or it may be as specific and technical as knowing how to discern special causes and common causes in process variation. A study conducted by Reeves and Bednar[1] in a large Veterans Administration hospital in the southwestern United States measured the perceived barriers to integrating quality management principles by top and middle managers in a large health care organization. They stated that understanding and promoting quality management concepts are essential for top and middle managers and are central to any organization's success with QMI integration in daily work. "Without appropriate and adequate *training*, employees will not have the *knowledge* and skills necessary to implement quality principles and practices." The Reeves and Bednar study of management perceptions of barriers to QMI is discussed later in this chapter.

Among the potential barriers, Woodland's senior staff were most concerned with their own and the staff's lack of knowledge and training. The need for knowledge and skill development was spontaneously identified multiple times in preproject surveys by 14 Woodland department heads in response to every open-ended question:

- Lack of training was identified as a "barrier to QMI acceptance in the work area" (4 of 14 responses).
- Providing education/in-service was listed as "actions senior staff can perform to show support for QMI" (3 of 14 responses).
- Providing education/in-service training would "support staff collaboration between departments" (3 of 14 responses).
- Education would be "one immediate action to help begin the QMI process" in each department (2 of 14 responses).

The 3-phase quality management integration process points to conducting an initial assessment in Phase 1 to gain an awareness of the current knowledge and understanding of quality management concepts among key individuals within the facility. This initial assessment provides some clues as to how to structure and design foundation quality management training.

Lack of Continual Training

Reeves and Bednar pointed out that "the most important and expensive part of a quality program, especially in the early stages, is training. . . . In instances where management has failed initially to devote sufficient funds to training, TQM programs have faltered and failed."[2] After QMI concepts become familiar and well established, true knowledge and understanding of these powerful tools and techniques provide a basis for interdepartmental collaboration. At that point, savings accelerate and reimburse organizations for the training time that they invested earlier in the process. After training, while concepts are fresh in their minds, all sectors of the organization must practice their new skills. Only then does the value of QMI become apparent to both employees and managers, as continuous improvement benefits them and improves their work life. It is important that training be applied in actual projects so that the benefits of QMI concepts are realized and the expense of training is justified.

Woodland's quality council proposed several projects following numerous discussions of the training that would be necessary and the costs of implementing it. Providing necessary resources requires discussion in every long-term care organization. The organization should anticipate that training costs will be the highest early in the QMI implementation effort, and the early cost savings then help to pay for subsequent QMI projects.

Beyond the overview–introduction level, ongoing training should provide experience in using the tools and techniques of QMI. Formal training may take place on the job or in a classroom environment. Informal training is provided through team activities or coaching by senior staff who themselves have been trained. Departmental quality improvement projects can provide informal QMI training for employees and one-to-one discussion and coaching between employees and managers. If top management expects management by fact, then the skills to do so require systematic planning and training.

The CQI training needs assessment mentioned in Phase 3 of the 3-phase quality management integration process is a useful tool to evaluate the knowledge and skill levels of staff and to identify training priorities. One of the core concepts of the QMI model is continual learning. Formal training is one of the ways to encourage all staff to enhance their knowledge, skills, and abilities continually to provide good-quality care and service.

Insufficient Empowerment by and Involvement of Middle Managers

Middle managers (department heads) may be afraid of the impact of QMI on their authority because "by definition, TQM requires that managers let subordinates suggest changes and make decisions to improve the work environment and processes."[3] In other words, employee involvement and empowerment are core concepts in QMI.

Woodland's administrator recognized that middle manager involvement was pivotal because the department heads' commitment would be demonstrated by a number of factors, including the amount of problem solving and research time provided, their communications and efforts to involve employees, and their subsequent follow-through and implementation of projects and suggestions from employees. The administrator had been part of another organization's unsuccessful attempt at implementing QMI, in which such middle manager involvement and "buy-in" were not obtained. The survey respondents at Woodland also identified many such issues before the QMI project began.

The quality improvement projects of each department illustrate a means for involving all middle managers and promoting commitment throughout the organization. Many benefits of participative management also were illustrated in the case study of Carver Health Care Center at the beginning of Chapter 3. When managers practice participative management, a "win–win" environment is established. Customers receive high-quality care and service because employees are able to focus on the needs of the customer as opposed to merely pleasing their manager.

Vivian Booker, an experienced administrator, stated[4]

> *Department heads need to have commitment to do problem-solving. They should encour-age line staff to be creative in problem-solving, because they can make decisions closer to the customer. Department heads often put problem solving to the back burner because they are not sure how to proceed. The definition of management used to be "decision-maker," but now it's "coach" or "facilitator." Managers should acknowledge that committing to QMI is easier said than done since their background and training did not encourage them to take time to work on customer service.*

Underdeveloped Commitment Throughout the Entire Organization

Individual employees perform services for internal and external customers, the services that together make up "health care." The degree of understanding and implementation of QMI concepts by all of the employees in the organization, including management, deter-mines whether employees on the front line, who deal with the four customer groups, are consciously aware of providing customer satisfaction in a constantly improving environ-ment. Unless QMI implementation occurs with active, visible senior management partic-ipation, however, improved results occur only in isolated pockets of the organization. For organization-wide transformations such as these, the QMI process requires active partici-pation among top-level managers because so many critical processes cut across de-partments, across shifts, or (perhaps) between facilities. The politics and turf battles that accompany these changes can be extremely stressful to organizations unless senior man-agement provides consistent, positive, and collaborative direction. A simple example is the difficulty of changing the cross-functional processes that comprise the paperwork trail that must medically and legally follow a resident. (External consultants often are called in to "heal" organizations that exhibit vacillating commitment. If called promptly, they may help avert these difficult situations.)

Reeves and Bednar found that middle managers' "greatest concern was apathy and lack of commitment by all employees in the medical center . . . also concerned about a possible lack of confidence in the TQM program. . . . It is critical that both managers and employees understand that implementing TQM is a long-term process and will not produce easy quick fixes."[5] Middle managers, frontline supervisors, and employees gain organization-wide commitment more easily when top management truly models flexi-bility and a willingness to change established procedures.

Rapid turnover and a lesser degree of professionalism in two groups, nursing assis-tants and dietary aides, make their commitment to QMI problematic. Studies have found that many employees in these groups, with lesser levels of career expectations or educa-tion, prefer not to take on more responsibility or challenge at their jobs. Silwal, Wagers, and Armstrong[6] postulated that these workers place little trust in authority figures, largely because their suggestions for change in the past often have met with unpleasant conse-quences or outright hostility. Lack of willingness to participate in decision making, therefore, actually may increase their willingness to leave the nursing facility. The study authors found that increased training in entry-level positions decreased the turnover rate.[6] Management's ability to supervise, direct, support, and involve nursing assistants, housekeeping staff, and dietary aides is critical to QMI implementation and should be carefully planned and monitored. Other incentives also must be sought to make QMI a win-win situation for these groups.

Because of high turnover and reluctance regarding employee involvement among some members of these groups, the facility's quality council must develop strategies for different groups of employees. One long-term care organization, for example, has made a policy decision to involve nursing assistants and dietary aides only in their natural work groups' problem-solving efforts at first; after they become comfortable with participating in process improvement, they may receive further training for cross-functional process improvement teams.

The basic issue is trust between leaders and their employees. Managers need to create an environment in which trust can develop through time. When QMI changes such as team participation are first implemented, the key for managers is to find a number of small successes early in the transition process and communicate them to the general staff with enthusiasm. Improvements and successes should be made obvious to all observers. For instance, one organization placed graphs showing process improvements in their break rooms to stimulate employee involvement and interaction. Another group used department-specific bulletin boards on which were tacked employees' process improvement suggestions to stimulate discussion with supervisors and one another.

All of the department heads at Woodland voiced concern about the future commitment of the entire staff. These concerns included fear and reluctance to change, poor motivation or attitude of senior staff or employees, the need for a positive attitude by senior staff and employees, and the need for senior staff collaboration between departments (see Appendix E for survey results). Several senior staff members openly discussed their discomfort with empowerment of employees or delegation by the senior staff to other employees. To develop commitment throughout the entire organization, department managers and frontline supervisors must consistently practice QMI principles.

As the win-win aspects of QMI are disseminated throughout the facility, employees and department heads begin to support this change in organizational paradigms. Senior staff must carefully communicate these aspects of QMI until the concepts are well established in the organizational culture. Only then will all staff understand how these changes support the organization's goals.

Politics/Turf Battles

"Extensive employee involvement encourages a multifunctional perspective to problem solving. In many organizations, one of the greatest barriers to TQM is the territorialism that has evolved over many years. Turf battles frequently frustrate TQM implementation and produce other dysfunctional consequences for both individuals and organizations."[7] The matrix reproduced in Table 4-1 can help an organization overcome this potential barrier to effective process improvement by recognizing the systematic, interdepartmental nature of long-term care systems. (Note that the QMI system itself is subject to measurement and CQI.)

Politics and turf battles were not identified as a barrier by Woodland's senior staff. Political issues and turf battles were discussed but never as a factor in QMI acceptance per se. Conceivably, this problem could arise later, particularly if a department or administrator who is committed to QMI should waver or vacillate at a later time. Many staff mentioned the need for interdepartmental collaboration and communication, however, citing progressive deterioration during multiple leadership changes. A number of people believed that interdepartmental communication had improved during the time span of the case study; a few did not. (This sort of gap or difference of opinion provides an opportunity for investigation by consultants or the facility's administrator.)

Inadequate Resources

Inadequate resources is a potential barrier that may reflect both constrained budgets at the department level and lack of commitment by top management and the executive board. With an ever-tightening reimbursement system, budgets in most long-term care facilities are limited. Small expenditures provide great satisfaction, however, and they often serve dual purposes. For example, the quality council and the communications team planned a staff party to celebrate Woodland's successful compliance survey results. This celebration underscores the administrator's proper perception that QMI is part of all activities, not only those with a formal continuous improvement intent. Studying the budget may show that initial team meeting time may fall under the training/education category, for example.

The top manager group in Reeves's and Bednar's study mentioned the time required for meetings and problem solving, but not as a top priority.[8] Woodland's department heads listed it as a top priority, however. The provision of time for QMI activities is a constant budgetary concern at all long-term care facilities. The difficulty of scheduling is an issue, but the expense of providing back-up personnel certainly requires creative and consistent attention by senior staff. It is particularly damaging if employees or managers receive competing messages about the use of their time in solving problems. Woodland's survey respondents mentioned a "willingness to be flexible: work different hours, etc." as actions that senior staff could perform to show their support for QMI. The expectations of the administrator and the quality council should be clear so that all department heads can be confident in their application of resources for quality management projects.

Inappropriate Reward/Incentive System

One controversial issue is whether to provide monetary rewards for employee involvement in process improvement or for improved results/outcomes of QMI. We encourage organizations not to rely on such tangible rewards (i.e., extrinsic motivators) that originate from outside the individual but to create an organizational culture that draws upon the intrinsic motivators that are within each individual's personality. This recommendation is based on our experience both within and outside health care and on many studies in the professional literature.

Intrinsic motivators include intangible but powerful motivators such as pride of workmanship; a sense of accomplishment from process improvements; being challenged to achieve the best level of performance; a sense of collaboration, contribution, and trust among team members; and recognition by other employees and management. Extrinsic

Table 4-1. A systematic approach to process improvement counteracts politics/turf battles

Long-term care facilities put in place many systems that interact and support one another. Departments may develop a possessive and protective feeling about their own processes. We encourage the multifunctional approach to solving problems mentioned earlier as an antidote to the territorialism, turf battles, and politics that may have developed. Your organization may find this format helpful both for brainstorming during the problem identification process and for laying out departmental responsibilities when you implement changes. Processes interrelate and form systems: Changes in a local department's work patterns may affect other departments' process outcomes as well.

System	Outcome measures (key indicators)	Processes	Departments involved
Marketing System			
Admission System			
Care Planning and Documentation System			
Medication Administration System			
Personal Care Delivery System			
Restorative Care System			
Meal Service System			
Discharge System			
Billing and Collections System			
Preventive Maintenance and Repair System			
Risk Management System			
Recruitment and Hiring System			
Employee Development System			
Performance Management System			
QMI			

motivators are successful incentives for short-term change and involvement but are less successful in bringing about long-term shifts in an organization's cultural climate. A system of small prizes as token gifts may stimulate excitement and involvement, particularly at the outset. The weakness of extrinsic motivators, however, is that they are subject to long-term inflation. In other words, rewards of increasing size are needed to maintain long-term commitment from employees, if rewards are the primary motivators for employee involvement.

The issue of incentives and rewards for department head involvement did not arise at Woodland Care Center, except in the general sense of professional growth and career paths. The senior staff were aware of the growing importance of QMI in the health care field and also anticipated the benefits of improved productivity and participation to their departments. These were the issues emphasized in all training and quality council discussions as well. As Reeves and Bednar stated, "Appropriate rewards provide incentives for employees to participate in quality improvement efforts and tangibly and visibly demonstrate top management's commitment."[9] What is "appropriate" should be formally addressed and agreed on by the facility's quality council. The recognition of successful employee efforts is one element of successful QMI implementation and should be considered in strategic planning and discussions by senior staff. Creative ideas such as providing flextime may stimulate excitement among employees. Recognition and appreciation ideas are detailed in the following:

> Monthly recognition luncheon for groups of employees who are celebrating birthdays or anniversaries
>
> Personal thank-you note from supervisor
>
> T-shirt with facility logo for employees who go "above and beyond"
>
> Article about an employee in the monthly facility newsletter
>
> A pin for years of service (e.g., 5, 10, 15, 20 years of employment)
>
> Monthly potluck lunches for staff
>
> Secret Pal program (employees have a "secret pal" to whom they secretly send little notes or gifts over a period of time)
>
> Gift certificates or movie passes when employee is "caught" providing excellent customer service
>
> Ice cream treats for employees on especially hot days
>
> Casual dress allowed on the last payday of every month
>
> A free meal voucher for an employee on his or her employment anniversary or birthday
>
> An appreciation day each month for a particular department

Ineffective Communications

Obviously, ineffective communications can affect the implementation of QMI at all levels in the organization. That the need for effective communications was listed in response to three out of four questions in Woodland's survey underscores how critical this issue is among groups who must support one another's work and who work with the same groups of residents and families. Among three different questions, communications issues were raised 22 times in addition to being mentioned in a number of open-ended, unaggregated responses. Communications issues clearly receive the most consensus as a potential barrier among Woodland's department heads. As a result, these issues should receive careful attention from any consultants and the facility's administrator. (Woodland's survey results are found in Appendix E.) In the period since the survey, however, these managers have dwelled more on the issue of time, which will always be a challenge, and less on the communications issue, which, presumably, they can affect much more directly. The importance of effective communications and initial communications activities at Woodland also were discussed in Chapter 3.

Ineffective Measurement Techniques and Use of Data

Although long-term care facilities may collect a lot of data, often there are no systems in place to view the data routinely and turn them into information. In a quality management environment solid data are critical to good decision making. It is equally important that data and information not be concentrated at the department-management level. When facilities begin involving staff in data collection and analysis, it is imperative that staff understand that the data will be used for improvement purposes and will not in any way be used against them. It is also important to have clear operational definitions of how the data are to be collected. An operational definition is a description, in quantifiable terms, of what to measure and the steps that are necessary to measure it consistently.

Indispensable to either the fee-for-service or managed care payment scheme in a quality management environment is measuring the components of the care process. Tracking current levels and trends identifies opportunities for the facility to provide improved health care, including measuring clinical outcomes, lengths of stay, and levels and trends of resident/family satisfaction. Precisely estimating facility cost levels and customer groups is particularly important in an environment of electronic data submission and the federal prospective payment system (PPS). (The PPS is detailed in Chapter 5 in the section on financial reimbursement systems.)

When top managers use management by fact processes for decision making, they require data collection for decision making. This expectation provides the best incentive for training and process improvement in the departments. The indicator priority matrix (Figure 4-1)[10] provides a method for considering which quality indicators are the best measures for systems and processes, enabling decision making by the quality council and senior management.

A reluctance to collect data is common in initial implementations of QMI; it also occurred at Woodland. Formal training is particularly effective in overcoming this attitude. Several of the senior staff at Woodland, who are nurses and therapists, stated that they are not "numbers people." They focus on individual residents and do not enjoy collecting data for the purpose of making decisions about systematic process improvements. Often, the explanation is lack of time, but discussion revealed that they also have not had experience collecting or analyzing data methodically or displaying the data graphically. Woodland's administrator mentioned that several department heads found one-to-one support with the consultant particularly helpful as they implemented new data collection concepts.

Guidance and modeling by the quality council is vital for developing commitment to management by fact and data-driven decision making throughout the organization. The council must identify the data systems and indicators that are essential for monitoring the quality of care and service provided within the facility. These data are routinely analyzed

Key: To what degree does each of these factors apply to your potential indicator? 5 = High application; 3 = moderate application; 1 = low application; 0 = no relevance.

Indicator	Do data already exist or are they easy to collect?	Is this measure already in place?	Does it measure high risk to customer or facility?	Critical to customer satisfaction?	Able to clearly define and measure	Has a problem already occurred?	Score
Admission documentation complete	5	3	1	2	3	0	14
No. of falls	5	5	5	3	3	3	24

Examples { (bracket spanning the two example rows)

Figure 4-1. Indicator priority matrix.

by the council to identify improvement needs. The following lists some considerations for determining which data to collect:

- Define the expected outcomes for the facility.
    Mission and vision of the facility
    What the facility's customers really care about
    Expected outcomes of key facility systems
- Identify the core processes and systems.
- Identify the organization's needs for data.
    Clinical outcomes and processes
    Quality of the service provided (satisfaction of customers)
    Financial indicators
    Human resources data
- Brainstorm to develop a list of potential indicators.
- Use the indicator priority matrix (Figure 4-1) to select among items in the brainstormed list of indicators.
- Identify the available data sources.
    Databases
    Surveys
    Logs
    Observational studies
- Develop data collection methods.

The same series of issues then cascades to the department level based on the organization's priorities and vision. Management by fact and the usefulness of effective data collection also are examined in detail in Chapter 6.

Poor Customer Focus

The word *customer* may not be accepted unequivocally by all staff members. To some, the word conjures pictures of a retail clerk interacting with a person in the checkout lane—friendly, perhaps, but superficial. In contrast, the relationship among care providers and residents and their families often grows deeper and more personal. Consequently, the word *customer* may generate some resistance from staff. The issue of defining internal and external customer relationships did arise at Woodland. The quality council and communications team both emphasized treating all of the residents as favored customers, and they discussed examples of residents who presented particular challenges to this intention.

A much greater barrier than perception, however, is not having systems in place to listen to customers. To overcome this barrier, the quality council must identify methods that will be used to gather and analyze customer data and then establish a way to carry that information to direct care and service providers to drive change. Channels that promote listening more closely to customers' needs and requirements may include the following:

- Suggestion systems
- Family focus groups and family satisfaction committees
- Complaint system that gathers and analyzes trends in customer dissatisfaction

- Surveys and interviews of families and residents or other customer groups (e.g., payer groups or regulatory agencies, physicians)
- Effective analysis of customer data using QMI tools and techniques (results of this analysis determine key satisfaction and dissatisfaction indicators to be established and tracked)

The behaviors and actions of direct care and services providers profoundly affect residents and families and strongly influence the perceived quality of the care and service provided. Training and customer orientation meetings equip employees with strong interpersonal and communication skills to build and maintain relationships with customers.

Management Perceptions of Barriers to QMI

Reeves and Bednar[11] examined and classified 11 issues that they identified as potential barriers to successful quality management implementation in health care (Table 4-2). These barriers have been cited in the professional literature on implementing TQM and CQI. All 11 issues were management's perceptions of barriers to quality management, *internal* to the organization. Reeves and Bednar then compared those literature-based results with real-life perceptions of top and middle managers in health care. We drew upon the barriers identified by Reeves's and Bednar's study as well as our own experience with quality management implementation in long-term care facilities when we developed our list of barriers internal to the long-term care facility. These 11 categories become barriers only if they are not addressed. For example, if the barrier "top managers' support" becomes a factor in the QMI process, then it will become a major bottleneck for implementation as a whole.

Reeves's and Bednar's study illustrates that levels of agreement about the potential barriers to TQM implementation that were identified from the professional literature can differ among groups of top and middle managers. Each barrier identified is analyzed in terms of whether it is prioritized by top managers or by middle managers. Agreement among all three categories occurs in only 4 of the 11 areas: top managers' support, long-term focus, commitment throughout the organization, and ineffective communication. These four issues truly are at the heart of any successful quality management implementation process. Reeves and Bednar summarized management's perception of the barriers as follows:[12]

> *The top managers' perceptions appear to reflect a more general and organizationwide orientation toward TQM implementation. . . . Middle managers were more concerned with the pragmatic and operational issues of implementation. . . . [For example,] Middle managers viewed adequate [sic] training as a potential barrier; top managers cited the more general problem of lack of understanding and knowledge of TQM. . . . [As is true in all TQM implementations,] both levels identified their direct supervisors as having the potential to present significant barriers to TQM implementation.*

All 11 barriers are under management control. Only when senior management and leadership groups change their expectations, redirect their allocation of resources, and remove all of the barriers are employees able to optimize changes to their workday processes and successfully implement QMI processes throughout their facility.

Table 4-2.   11 barriers to QMI implementation—management's perceptions

Barrier	Identified in literature	Prioritized by	
		Top managers	Middle managers
Top managers' support	x	x	x
Incentives and rewards	x	x	
Long-term focus	x	x	x
Training	x		x
Commitment throughout organization	x	x	x
Middle managers' involvement	x		
Vision	x		
Politics/turf battles	x		x
Inadequate resources	x		x
Ineffective communication	x	x	x
Inadequate knowledge/ understanding	x	x	

Different Management Groups Hold Different Perceptions of the Internal Barriers to QMI

Because Reeves's and Bednar's study focused on identifying barriers in the literature and comparing them with perceptions of a fairly large management group of 79 top and middle managers, issues of quality management implementation were shown to differ between the two management subgroups. Their differing perceptions may have a strong impact on decisions that are implemented at different organizational levels:[13]

> *The perceived meaning of generic obstacles, such as inadequate resources and lack of management support, varied across management levels. Failure to accurately define and specifically differentiate these barriers across hierarchical levels can hinder effective TQM implementation. . . . The traditional style of health care organization management, however, produces many obstacles to effective TQM implementation. By understanding the perceived barriers, health care executives can more precisely define and anticipate problems impeding effective TQM implementation.*

The typical long-term care facility such as Woodland will employ a smaller staff than the facility studied by Reeves and Bednar, so hierarchical issues may not be as clear-cut. Nevertheless, quality professionals and administrators should be sensitive to the differing needs and interests of individual managers at various levels in the organizational hierarchy.

Other Critical Issues

Two internal issues that are not solely management issues also may become barriers and may strongly influence your QMI success: 1) gaining support from physicians is central to all clinical process improvement, and 2) understanding the family as a system is essential to holistic care.

Gaining Support from Physicians

Gaining physician support for quality management is a management issue that is discussed frequently in the professional literature. Physicians can resist and even sabotage efforts for process change if they do not understand its benefits. Although they may not be administrators, physicians certainly manage the care processes with which they are involved. This authority is derived from their experience, their high level of responsibility, and their professional training. Successful quality management implementation eventually requires involvement of the medical staff, despite any resistance, ideally in team activities focused on their own processes.

Long-term care facilities tend to be less controlled by groups of doctors than are hospitals, and physicians have more contact with the organization on an individual basis, depending on their patients' needs. For example, Woodland Care Center has contracted with a medical director who becomes involved in discussions with individual doctors when the staff and administrator believe that it is necessary. He chairs the quality assurance committee, which is mandated by state regulations and includes agenda items identified by the administrator. It is not typical for a medical director to chair the quality assurance committee, however. Facilities benefit most from QMI when the medical director takes some sort of active role in the quality council. For an active QMI leadership role, the medical director and other doctors require further knowledge and understanding of QMI. Physicians may be especially helpful when the quality council is working with technical quality tools, such as interpreting quality management data and trends.

Based on their backgrounds as nursing facility administrators, both Vivian Booker[14] and Thomas Stofac[15] agree that eventually a medical director's role should focus on process improvements to ensure consistent, high-quality clinical outcomes for residents. They envision physicians providing a clinical focus within the quality council or a process improvement committee, which should merge the old quality control/quality assurance paradigms with new process and systems management concepts. Because they are comfortable with data analysis, medical directors and other physicians play an important role in coaching team members and management in the analysis and interpretation of metrical indicators for care processes. In particular, working with process data over a period of time (common cause data) rather than at a single point in process performance should be encouraged.

Some quality management improvement processes begin with business and administration areas and others with frontline care processes, but eventually QMI involves all areas, including physicians. All facilities must consider physician representation an issue in their quality management implementation. Because reimbursement for their time may become an issue, communication of the win–win situation for physicians is key. Involve them when their presence is of value to them as well as to the QMI process, for example when dealing with clinical data at executive level meetings. Traditionally, it was accepted that in nursing facilities physicians do not drive care, but with the trend toward subacute units for shorter-term convalescent care they are increasingly involved in decision making and spend a great deal of time with their patients in the facilities. Thus, physicians should play an active role in all three segments of Juran's quality trilogy (quality planning, quality control, and quality improvement; see Chapter 2) to stay current with facility changes and decision making. Physician representation on the quality council achieves that end. (A fine resource for physician and senior management education in QMI principles and practices is the Institute for Healthcare Improvement in Boston; see Appendix J.)

Understanding the Family as a System

Unlike acute care environments, which generally deal with short-term episodes of care, long-term care facilities often care for residents through long periods of time. Thus it is imperative for long-term care providers to recognize the impact of the resident's family system on care planning. It is to the providers' benefit to educate both residents and family members about the goals of rehabilitation, health maintenance, and maximal independence for residents. Hence, customer satisfaction data collection should include both residents and their families and caregivers. Satisfaction surveys should address some areas for families as a separate customer group; for example, what are their unique needs? Data collection tests whether quality improvement projects result in long-term successful outcomes for both of these customer groups.

Demographic changes are bringing younger, posthospital, rehabilitative patients to nursing facilities. Younger, short-term residents tend to be more independent as decision makers (they are less dependent on surrogate decision makers such as family or caregivers) and require different types of support processes from facility staff. This group already has brought major revisions in strategic quality planning for customers at Woodland and other long-term care facilities. These changes will accelerate as the long-term care industry evolves and becomes more vertically integrated.

Quality Management from the Corporate Perspective

When an organization with multiple facilities decides to implement QMI, quality leadership and quality councils address a number of complex issues beyond those within the single facility (see Figure 3-1 for an illustration of a sample infrastructure in a multifacility organization). Many policy decisions regarding quality management must be made centrally. Then senior management practices should support effective management practices in all units. For example, "Quality management should be blended into Quality Assurance and department head meetings, so that they are all 'quality,'" according to Deborah Perry, Director of Mission Fulfillment at Volunteers of America (VOA) Health Services.[16] Examples of corporate considerations that require strategic planning for the multifacility organization follow:

- How much consistency is required between units, in training, in tracking data, in team structures, and so forth?
- How much support will be provided from the corporate level, and how much reporting to the executive level is required?
- Will successful implementations be slowed or even halted to allow other facilities to catch up?
- When long-term care facilities are affiliated with other health care providers, through mergers, health maintenance organizations, managed care providers, or other associations, what

issues may need to be addressed? (Human resources issues such as staff anxiety need to be addressed along with any major policy/procedure shifts.)

- The needs assessments of Phase 1 in the 3-phase quality management integration process also should be performed for the larger organization through the corporate office quality council and at the facility level.
- Process improvements at all levels use the same QMI tools, such as the 3-phase quality management integration process and the PDSA cycle.

The importance of ownership of the QMI process within individual facilities is clear. In a multifacility organization, however, oversight of the organization-wide QMI effort is monitored at a corporate level. (Woodland Care Center planning included corporate vocabulary and QMI concepts in initial overviews and training.) Momentum should be monitored or reported, but each facility's senior staff provide leadership for their own departments, depending on their own facility's culture. Several ways to encourage facility participation and ownership (decentralization), for example, would be for senior staff to benchmark with one another and share data and successful process improvements among themselves. It is vital that ownership of projects and processes remains under individuals and departments, and not under external consultants, internal consultants, corporate executives, or even individual administrators. Many printed materials are common across the corporation for purposes of communicating corporate name, mission, and record of service. Similarly, some QMI processes and policies may be held in common. Various corporate considerations, including guidance by the corporate quality council, are detailed in the following:

1. Philosophy and Vision: Developing an organization-wide quality management philosophy and vision provides clear direction and a set of guiding principles to all of the facilities within the organization. From this common philosophy and vision, each facility can define how these values will be carried out in its setting to achieve the desired outcomes.

2. Corporate Quality Council: Establishing a corporate quality council creates an infrastructure that supports the organization-wide integration of quality management and sustains the philosophy. In addition to corporate staff, representation from the board and facility levels to provide a multilevel perspective to the QMI process should be considered. The primary focus of this council is to establish and steer the quality improvement system, including organization-wide training, data collection and analysis, process improvement, and reward and recognition for the enhancement of quality care and services. The council directs corporate resources to prioritized quality management activities that further the organization's mission, vision, and philosophy in a cascading system down to local sites. A robust communications system to ensure linkages among all local sites and the central offices may be one of the quality council's most important contributions to QMI.

3. Organizational Outcomes Monitoring: Corporate staff should define a set of key outcome measurements that provide a way to track organization-wide patterns and trends and to measure improvement progress. What outcomes should be measured? Key corporate outcomes generally arise from the responses to two questions: 1) What do the customers of the organization really care about? and 2) What is the strategic direction that will ensure future success for the organization? Outcome measures may include customer satisfaction or dissatisfaction and clinical, operational, financial, and human resources indicators. (For lists of key indicators that provide possi-

ble comparative data between facilities, and perhaps with competitors, and for examples of graphing key processes over time on run charts, see Chapter 6.)

4. Common Improvement Process and Language: As there are several different approaches to process improvement, a common improvement process and language among facilities should be created so that communication between facilities is maximized. Whether it is called QMI, TQM, or CQI or whether a 10- or a 7-step problem-solving process is used, standard methodology and terminology allow shared learning among and between facilities.

5. Board of Directors' Involvement: Involvement on the part of the board of directors is essential to ensure ongoing financial support. If quality management is not a board initiative, then the board needs to be educated regarding the philosophy, framework, and benefits of quality management. Search for board members who have quality improvement expertise.

6. Best Practices: How can process improvements be shared throughout the organization? When processes are enhanced in one facility, it makes sense to share those successes with other facilities in the organization. Consider establishing a system that efficiently communicates best practices from facility to facility. Some organizations hold an annual quality fair to showcase success stories, providing recognition for successful projects and sharing effective quality approaches among facilities.

7. Local Autonomy: Questions that frequently arise in multifacility organizations are what needs to be centralized and what needs to be standardized through the organization? What should be under the authority of the individual facility? When these questions are not answered, both corporate staff and facility staff become frustrated. Clarify up front what will be standardized and what will not. For example, a standard might be that all of the facilities in the organization establish a quality council. What is not standardized is that the composition of the council may be up to the individual facilities.

Mature corporate QMI processes may include interfacility teams on topics such as care planning, staffing, and scheduling. These are broad issues for single facilities to address, and, often, they have legal repercussions. Some common training is helpful at the beginning to ensure common direction, process expectations, and vocabulary. Pilot projects are important because they allow small-scale implementations to test suggested process improvements, which was the corporate plan for Woodland's national organization. The important strategic guidance of the governing board is illustrated in the display on page 76.

Summary

Make no mistake—implementing QMI is a challenge, but successful implementations can be found in every type of long-term care facility, whether for profit or not-for-profit and whether single facility or multifacility chain. Some organizations are open to the culture changes brought by QMI implementation; others are uncomfortable with the concepts of CQI (continual change) and TQM (involving all employees, even the CEO, in organizational transformation and process improvement). Active consideration of the potential internal barriers and critical issues examined in this chapter help ensure success.

Unlike decision makers in many other industries, health care providers often make decisions under stress, when only partial information is available. Thus, establishing consistent, reproducible, effective processes, including documentation, should be a primary

Strategic Quality Planning Begins with the Board of Directors and Flows Through the Organization

The board of directors or governing board typically is involved in defining a vision for the organization, creating strategies to reach the vision, and outlining company policies. When engaging in these activities, board members should consider the core concepts of quality management, especially the concepts of customer focus and systems thinking. Clearly, the members of the board must have an understanding of quality management principles beyond a basic level, if they are to lead the process effectively.

The Board of Directors of the national organization Volunteers of America (VOA) made the decision to move beyond monitoring facility compliance with regulatory standards (quality assurance) to becoming proactive through the use of QMI. The board directed staff to explore quality management models and to learn how these concepts might be implemented within VOA. A task force was established and, working with an external consultant, a needs assessment was conducted.

Pilot projects were begun at three sites. Some of the components of the initial process were

- ◆ Establishment of department teams for improvement and monitoring of processes
- ◆ Resident satisfaction, monitored through interview surveys of families and designated caregivers
- ◆ Interdepartmental process improvement teams

The project's findings in all three areas were positive. The corporate quality management task force agreed on various improvements and modifications before expanding the process to all of the facilities.

The three project sites administered the quality-of-life assessment survey to collect data on residents' levels of satisfaction from the residents' designated caregivers and families. One surprise finding was that the residents' primary dissatisfaction, as expressed through this surrogate group, was with physician services, as compared with scores for other answers. As facilities have little control over this area, results were simply communicated to physicians through the facilities' medical directors, and results were posted. Deborah Perry, Director of Mission Fulfillment of VOA,[16] noted that if the question had not been asked, the higher level of dissatisfaction would not have been recognized or communicated. It is to be expected that residents and families always will desire more contact with physicians. Two responses, however, may be to improve communications through the facility's other care providers and to educate residents to hold more realistic expectations for their interactions with physicians.

Another example of corporate strategic role is in the facility's relationship with the corporate office. Perry explained:

> *The Board should remain knowledgeable about each facility's marketing and community research, but the facilities should then manage their own initiatives, showing their willingness to partner and share risks in viable affiliations with other organizations. Rural communities have very different needs from metropolitan areas with heavily managed care environments.*

To expand the dissemination of information and techniques, Perry promotes the development of intercorporate groups. These groups would reach beyond the VOA system to share materials such as training formats and content or noncompetitive benchmarking data or process improvements. The governing board must address these types of strategic decisions.

focus for senior managers. Understanding management by fact and the importance of common cause versus special cause occurrences is essential for department heads and supervisors, as is an unerring sense of residents' long-term needs.

The QMI model, with its six core concepts and its emphasis on using data for decision making, and the 3-phase quality management integration process guide a facility's quality journey. They provide the vision that helps managers identify and address the internal barriers and critical issues that otherwise might hinder the organization's implementation of QMI.

References

1   Reeves, C.A., & Bednar, D.A. (1993, April). What prevents TQM implementation in health care organizations? *Quality Progress,* 41. (Emphasis added)

2   Ibid., p. 41.

3   Ibid., p. 41.

4   Booker, V. (1994). Personal communication.

5   Op cit., pp. 41, 43.

6   Silwal, R., Wagers, K., & Armstrong, C. (1994). *Analysis of CNA (certified nursing assistants) turnover in two Saint Paul nursing homes* (p. 20). Unpublished manuscript.

7   Reeves & Bednar, p. 42.

8   Ibid., p. 43.

9   Ibid., p. 41.

10   The quality council first identifies, by brainstorming, the potential indicators in key processes that could be measured. Next, council members measure the relevance of each criterion against each indicator, applying a numeric value or weight. The values are then added to determine which of the indicators carry the greatest total weight. This process can be used by a facility-wide quality council or multifacility organization as well as by individual departments.

11   Op cit., pp. 41–44.

12   Ibid., pp. 41–43.

13   Ibid., p. 44.

14   Booker, V. (1994). Personal communcation.

15   Stofac, T. (1994). Personal communication.

16   Perry, D. (1995). Personal communication.

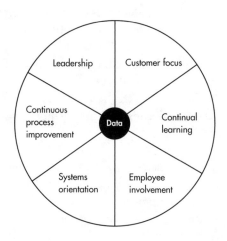

Chapter 5

EXTERNAL CRITICAL ISSUES

Chapter 4 examined many of the barriers to successful integration of quality management principles within the culture and processes of the long-term care organization. Appropriate responses were detailed for each of the problematic behaviors and attitudes. Pressures on the long-term care organization also arise from outside the facility, requiring managers and employees to remain flexible and respond promptly. These external critical issues require careful attention; the process control and timely responses of quality management integration (QMI) will minimize their impact on customer service and facility operations.

Reimbursement and regulatory systems are external to the institution and are directed by government bureaucracies and payer groups such as insurance companies. These systems become a barrier to QMI when management uses them as a justification for avoiding the challenge of transforming the leadership/management process in health care organizations. Management can work within the limitations of reimbursement and regulatory conditions, but management's acceptance of the status quo and a compliance mentality can inhibit organizational transformation. Regulatory standards should be viewed as minimum levels, and process measurement and improvement should enable a facility to achieve, at increasing levels, effective, efficient process performance.

Financial Reimbursement Systems

Long-term care facilities are reimbursed through federal and state governments' Medicare/Medicaid programs, through the private resources of residents, or through managed care programs such as health maintenance organizations (HMOs). HMOs estimate their costs through a *capitation* process, which is based on estimated average costs of health care per person per month.

Fee-for-Service Reimbursements

Because care in the traditional fee-for-service model reimburses at a higher level based on more skilled and costly care, health care facilities often are unintentionally biased to provide residents with these more expensive care modalities. This bias may promote the use of updated facilities, expensive new technology, and more specialized nursing care and rehabilitation programs. There is no financial incentive to make the resident independent; reimbursement levels have been determined based on historical costs of care. Clinical outcomes for the residents suffer, however, in that residents may stay sick, become increasingly dependent, and maximize days in the institution. Former long-term care administrator Thomas Stofac stated,[1]

> Reimbursement systems in many states provide no rehabilitation incentive. Quality of service delivery is measured by incorrect criteria. Organizations may be reimbursed for an increased level of activity, not for providing effective health care and rehabilitation outcomes. In effective health care processes, either fee-for-service or managed care, TQM/CQI implementation should provide better balance between cost and quality outcomes.

Prospective Payment System

The prospective payment system (PPS), one of the results of the Balanced Budget Act of 1997, was established by the U.S. Congress as a means of controlling the costs of Medicare-covered services. The system eliminates cost reimbursement and routine cost limits for Medicare days in skilled nursing facilities. Instead, rates under this system are fixed, regardless of the actual cost of the service. This places the financial risk on the provider and creates a strong incentive for the provider to control costs. Using QMI tools and techniques, the long-term care organization has a more accurate assessment of processes and their outcomes, as driven by their common cause systems.

Using the Minimum Data Set (MDS) resident assessment tool, a grouping system takes the assessment information and combines diagnostic and medical information with information on the physical and mental functioning of individual residents. Payments are made for Medicare-covered residents based on their individual case-mix grouping result. (See Chapter 6 for additional information about the MDS.) With the MDS serving as the foundation for determining a resident's case-mix placement, facilities need to ensure accurate and timely documentation by all levels of staff and have the proper computer hardware and software systems to ensure correct grouping and transmission of data. Staff must complete the MDS on a 5-, 14-, 30-, and 90-day schedule. If the information is not submitted at the correct intervals, then payment is made at the lowest default rate. In addition, if the documentation is not accurate and complete, facilities lose payments that they are entitled to receive.

The scores from the completed MDS determine resident placement in 1 of 44 resource utilization groups, also known as RUGs. The RUG classification system groups residents according to their care needs. Each RUG corresponds with an established per diem payment rate. The higher the RUG classification, the higher the payment. Therefore, the timely and accurate completion of the MDS is the first step toward ensuring that a facility's costs will be met in caring for its residents. It is crucial that the nursing staff understand how the RUG classification system works because these groupings and their corresponding payment rates have a direct impact on reimbursement and the bottom line.

Managed Care Systems

Managed care programs, which are based on actuarial rates, are the smallest segment of long-term care reimbursement but are growing the most quickly. Managed care may rely on QMI processes and principles to ensure that effective processes result in successful long-term outcomes and minimized risk. Managed care tends to minimize institutionalization and to lower costs, which are gauged on an institutional days used per 1,000 population basis, that is, efficiency of the care process. Regardless of diagnosis, such organizations want to bring residents to a healthy state and maintain them there, again to minimize costs. Such residents often come to long-term care from acute care facilities such as hospitals and may not stay at the facility after short-term rehabilitation. Thus, most facilities are treating a somewhat different population in need of a higher level of care for a shorter period of time. Patients who stay in hospitals tend to use more services than those who do not; managed care, therefore, manages convalescent costs better at nursing facilities with their lower cost levels. Following their stay, residents may then return home or go to group living or other less-expensive noninstitutional living arrangements. The lines that separate acute care, long-term care, and community-based services are less clear. Institutional networks and affiliations and outright mergers of health care organizations reflect these trends. Nursing facility residents should benefit as a result, as the goals of speedy, effective rehabilitation are more clearly defined and facilities are rewarded with a greater market share of their chosen segment of the resident population. For instance, organizations, as a necessary outcome of their strategic planning process, may choose to focus on their particular organizational strengths and provide long-term care services in rehabilitation and therapies, dementia, short-term subacute care, or other focus area.

Resident Protection Under Managed Care

Potential drawbacks to managed care may include overly abbreviated institutional stays, less-sophisticated care because of cost minimization, and reduced interest in the resident population as individual personalities. How is the resident protected under managed care? Regulatory requirements are used to help maintain standards. More important, it is in the HMO's interest to ensure the continued health of the customer population. Thus, HMOs should minimize costs while maximizing successful clinical outcomes and customer satisfaction, the core intent of QMI implementation in health care.

Stofac is convinced not only that the general population will thrive under a fully developed capitated health care system but that quality improvement processes are necessary to ensure the best possible clinical outcomes and rehabilitation while minimizing costs.[1] A balance of cost and quality outcome measures should provide both the best care for each individual and optimal results for the organization. He also stresses the heavy impact of fines that may be leveled against organizations that are out of compliance. Tracking processes and outcomes with QMI techniques can help avoid such fines or risk of decertification by providing documentation and/or warning of process change. Risk management using outcomes and process data is a necessity in the health care delivery industries of the 1990s and beyond.

Vivian Booker, a long-term care administrator, agrees that the reimbursement system often does not reward use of total quality management (TQM):[2]

> *Long-term care organizations need to consider both aggregate costs and clinical results for their residents. Facilities should avoid duplicating assessments or treatments by several therapy departments or nursing areas. For example, large savings probably can occur by evaluating and reducing pharmaceutical costs or by transitioning required managed care to nursing assistants from therapists earlier than was done in the past. Identifying and measuring key processes that flow across an entire facility can harness the powerful tools of CQI and TQM to reduce costs and focus staff activities most effectively.*

When therapists achieve a certain desired level of care with a resident, they can team with the nurses and nursing assistants to plan and maintain the resident's care program. This provides a team approach to managing care rather than a separation of control into individual departments. Similarly, a corporate organization or HMO may consider co-treatment of residents through several networked facilities. Thus, redundant costs are eliminated, care is provided in an effective and consistent manner, and resident/family satisfaction is enhanced.

Regulatory Requirements

The U.S. government's efforts to assess the success of resident care models, particularly since the nursing facility reform legislation of the Omnibus Budget Reconciliation Act (OBRA) of 1987 (PL 100-203; see Appendix H for background information on OBRA and the regulatory process), have barely affected health care paradigms, largely because of slow implementation of changes in the survey or surveyor training processes. The compliance decision-making process itself displays variation in its interpretation by different surveyors. This inconsistency of interpretation by surveyors is monitored when federal surveyors conduct "look-behind" surveys. (See the display on page 83 for a description of the survey process and requirements.)

The overwhelming impact of the annual survey process was illustrated in Chapter 4 in its effect on Woodland Care Center. Primary customers—the residents and their families—became secondary as the needs of regulatory agencies dominated the attention of Woodland staff, particularly the department heads. Woodland focused on the surveyors' activities round-the-clock for a week and devoted a great deal of energy for several weeks afterward in response to survey findings. To displace the goals of resident care for such a large block of time is not productive for achieving the organization's mission.

One of the strongest arguments for implementation of QMI processes is precisely targeted on their benefits to residents and staff. By improving and documenting the care process through QMI, processes perform effectively and consistently, whether or not surveyors are on the premises. Thus, potential deficiencies are identified and corrected before

Maintaining Compliance

Purpose of the Survey Process

The long-term care facility's quality management process is under the scrutiny of the Health Care Finance Administration (HCFA). The goal of HCFA, through its surveying process, is to ensure that facilities can monitor themselves through their own quality assurance (QA) program. HCFA wants to know that if a facility has problems, its administration has indeed put in place a system that can identify, analyze, and resolve the problems through internal processes. HCFA and state surveyors do not want to act as the facility's QA program.

Survey Requirements

HCFA's basic requirements are the following:

- ◆ The quality assessment and assurance committee must meet at least quarterly.
- ◆ Members of the committee must include, at a minimum, the director of nursing, a physician designated by the facility, and at least three facility staff members. Some states have more stringent requirements, such as including the facility medical director on the committee.

As a part of the standard survey process, surveyors examine a facility's QA system by asking QA committee members and facility staff the following:

- ◆ Whether they have a QA committee
- ◆ How the QA committee identifies QA issues and activities
- ◆ How the QA committee responds to quality deficiencies
- ◆ What method the QA committee uses to evaluate its own effectiveness when it responds to deficiencies

If surveyors feel a facility has actual or probable quality deficiencies, they probe further to find out whether the QA team:

- ◆ Identified the quality deficiencies found by the surveyors
- ◆ Developed a plan to resolve those deficiencies
- ◆ Evaluated or has plans to evaluate the effectiveness of the planned interventions

The surveyors' goals are to determine whether the facility has a QA committee that has a plan in place to address quality concerns. They also want to ensure that staff are familiar with the process and its procedures.

---

surveyors arrive at the facility. QMI provides process improvement and documentation, thereby ensuring stable process outcomes. The QMI process also provides long-term care facilities with documentation that may serve to counter surveyors' claims of deficiencies. Appendix G contains a sample of an organization's strategic planning process for QMI that was developed specifically to satisfy new survey requirements, taking OBRA regulations into account.

Financial Reimbursement and Regulatory Standards

Because financial reimbursement is conditional on meeting regulatory standards, a quality assurance mindset that barely meets required standards, as opposed to a continuous process improvement mindset, may result. Such regulations may both inhibit process improvement in direct care areas and slow the implementation of continuous improvement in administrative areas. In other words, standards may become ceilings, not floors; facilities often interpret standards as optimal targets, not as minimum acceptable performance. It is proper that standards are set for reimbursement, but these measurements of successful care may encourage some institutions to maintain the status quo to ensure payment rather than to take legitimate steps toward refinement and advancement. Financial reimbursement systems illustrate the power and influence of the important payer and regulatory agency customer groups.

The intent of OBRA was to make the system resident centered and outcome oriented and to assess whether resident outcomes were consistent with both regulatory requirements and intended outcomes of residents' health care plans. In the interest of cost containment, for example, many state policies attempt to promote maintaining individuals in a healthier state and at longer and lower levels of care. Unfortunately, survey processes may promote meeting standards, not exceeding them, and may be interpreted to measure facility success with factors that do not require continuous process improvement. Furthermore, facility managers' performance may be gauged and rewarded according to these standards.

Drawbacks to the survey system were clearly defined and quantified in the 1994 *Level A Compliance Decision Making Report* from the Foundation of the American College of Health Care Administrators. (Level A deficiencies are deficiencies that are the most significant and most damaging to the long-term care facility.) The Foundation's report used scientific methodology and a random survey process to examine 48 major Level A HCFA surveys from 17 states; the sample is representative of states (57%) and regions (87%). Data were analyzed both quantitatively and qualitatively. Citation rates and error rates (compliance decision not justified) were examined. The findings showed that 33% of major Level A citations were not justified; 44% of the survey teams did not follow HCFA rules, and the survey process may not be reliable to facilitate consumer protection. The report stated that "sanctions and penalties under 'enforcement' regulations may be harmful to some good facilities."[3,4] The project team reported that people should learn that they can challenge the system when they can document their claims. The report's conclusions included the following:

- Noncompliance decision making when citing Level A citations is not reliable in the application of frequency, in consideration of severity, and in following and applying the HCFA survey protocols.
- The consideration and application of key elements of the survey process used as factors in substantiating noncompliance at Level A are not uniformly reliable when evaluated by the written documentation in HCFA-2567.
- Reliability in noncompliance decisions, which is critical for the professional administrator, for standard disciplines and sanctions by various licensure boards and for the licensed practicing professionals working in nursing facilities, is lacking.[3]

The report's conclusion proposed the following criteria for successful OBRA improvements:

The Foundation and the project team offer seven recommendations as a result of these findings. The team hopes that the information will be of assistance in the full implementation of the OBRA promise.

   1. Written survey rules must be followed.

   2. Accountability must be created for invalid compliance decisions.

   3. Survey complexity must be reduced.

4. *Accurate and consistent citation decision making should be ensured.*
5. *The movement to outcomes, resident-centered decisions, and current clinical practice standards must be accelerated.*
6. *Effective dispute resolution must be ensured to promote accuracy and consistency nationwide.*
7. *Nationwide uniformity in compliance decision making is mandatory for consumer protection and quality assurance.*[4]

In effect, the report proposed improving the compliance and survey process in terms that could—and should—apply to most regulated industries and organizations as well as to health care. Although the study was completed in 1994, many of the problems remain.

A Picture of the Future: Integrated Delivery Systems

Relationships and networks of health care facilities among doctors, hospitals, nursing facilities, and community-based living are developing rapidly. All of these groups provide care for older adults who can no longer maintain their independence and for people requiring temporary convalescent subacute care, who make up a growing proportion of the residents in a long-term care facility. In health care these new integrated delivery systems (IDSs; see the exhibit on p. 86) rely on QMI tools and techniques to promote a flexible response to the new health care environment and to meet rising customer expectations of continually improved levels of care. Furthermore, an increasing share of this network, including Woodland Care Center, is addressing the requirements of managed care systems and traditional fee-for-service groups. Woodland and its national parent organization are being forced to redefine their mission, their customer groups, and their services to meet the needs of customers in this new marketplace.

> *These new systems of alliances, joint ventures, and mergers among healthcare providers are transforming the way healthcare companies across America deliver care. Once disparate, intensely competitive corporate elements are joining forces in these IDSs to offer residents—and payers—one-stop shopping for their healthcare needs . . .*
>
> *In recent years, virtually every major long-term care company in America has joined the rush toward integration, establishing alliances with other healthcare providers such as hospitals, subacute care providers, assisted living ventures and home care agencies. The goal is to participate in a network of services that spans the continuum of care, stretching from hospital to home. "I think it's pretty clear to us that, in a five- or 10-year horizon, most healthcare will be provided though an integrated delivery system," says William Eggbeer, vice president for marketing with Manor Healthcare, a $1-billion-a-year operation. "The rate of evolution varies a lot from market to market, but it's definitely the wave of the future."*[6]

The IDSs, also called integrated service networks (ISNs), are under consideration by most long-term care and health care facilities. Typically, informal or formal arrangements are in place with networks of physicians, hospitals, long-term care facilities such as Woodland, and others. To compete financially or for market share, these considerations must be ad-

Organizational Impact of Vertically Integrated Systems on Employees

As changes occur in the competitive marketplace, regulatory and payer groups, and customer expectations, the long-term care industry is responding with many shifts in organization structures and strategic plans. The emotional impact on employees and customers alike makes professional life in long-term care facilities both challenging and less than secure. Employees, including management, fear the unknown, such as mergers, management and staff turnover, shifts in marketing focus, and, especially, reduced quality of care for residents. In such a tense and anxiety-producing atmosphere, managers and staff may be unwilling to invest time or effort in long-term changes and improvements such as QMI. Short-term projects seem to offer more immediate rewards.

The risks that accompany newly developed IDSs, for example, cause great stress for health care employees. The biggest source of anxiety in formal mergers or networks is the loss of an organizational identity and culture without knowledge of what will develop to replace it. Employee concerns also include issues such as "What will happen to my job?" "What new tasks will I perform, and what standards and requirements will change?" and "How will my income be affected?" Realistically, redundancies are likely to develop with mergers, and potential job effects are likely.

Having guided organizations through mergers and other transitions, Stofac[1] described these losses of identity and culture and accompanying stressors in terms of employees' concerns. Typically, senior management knows what it believes to be the concerns of these groups, and it knows what its own assessments are, but frequently questions from the staff are not encouraged and are not answered openly. Questions occur at all levels of the organization; in larger organizations, middle-level managers are highly vulnerable. Thus, Stofac discussed people's need to know in terms of the feedback mechanisms that are provided by management. Good communications systems may include

- Surveys and focus groups that provide forums for discussion and questioning
- Training and communications that specifically respond to employee and manager queries
- Published memoranda and question-and-answer publications that can relay information quickly
- Middle managers and supervisors who are kept updated, so they can allay both employee concerns and their own anxieties (e.g., at breakfast forums with the CEO)

It is vital that these communications be two-way communications so that productivity is affected as little as possible and so that senior management provides the timely, accurate information that employees need.

To develop an IDS in an organization dedicated to QMI, certainly there should be another component. A system should be in place to assess the success of this communications process, as with other processes. This system should ask the following questions:

- Who are the customer groups for the IDS information?
- How successful is the communications delivery process?
- Are the customers satisfied?

Outside the typical financial and bureaucratic concerns, management groups in long-term care facilities are or will be responsible for leading their organizations into new health care structures and environments, inflicting minimal impact on their primary customer groups, the residents and their families. Successful organizational changes often are guided by dedicated transition teams that pinpoint problem areas and anticipate roadblocks.[5]

dressed. Nevertheless, managers must acknowledge and address the risks in these new affiliations as well.

Because these systems are in a state of flux, strategic quality planning is overturned constantly by new decisions among various groups of customers or competitors. As these rapid changes accelerate and organizations strive to position themselves as care providers, QMI data on trends and performance levels become even more vital for top managers and strategic planners.

Barriers and Critical Issues (Internal and External)

The *Sterling Review Newsletter* details "roadblocks which slow or detour progress".[7] The discussion of roadblocks serves to summarize and elaborate many barriers and critical issues, both internal and external, that are discussed here and in Chapter 4.

1. *Policies [established primarily] for facility convenience and control*
2. *Overspecialization/departmental barriers*
3. *Service process uncoordinated*
4. *Remote policy and decision making*
5. *Arbitrary service policies*
6. *Top priority on cost containment*
7. *Indifferent, unmotivated, powerless staff*
8. *Minimal creative problem solving*
9. *Lack of listening to customers*
10. *Focus on fixing, not preventing, problems*
11. *Frontline workers powerless to solve problems*
12. *Overpromising to customers*

Knowing what customers expect is the first and possibly most critical step in delivering quality service. Many facilities miss the mark by thinking inside out (they presume to know what customers should want and deliver that) rather than outside in (listening with an open mind).

Living in a long-term care environment means more than receiving adequate medical or technological care if the environment attempts to simulate homelike qualities. Of particular importance is the quality of the hundreds of daily interactive moments between residents and individual staff members. Yet most measurements gauge regulatory compliance rather than customer satisfaction.

The primary external customers of long-term care are the resident, family, and other designated responsible parties. They are the immediate end users of the services and the beginning point at which to begin quality improvement. In order to stay focused on the end users, it is desirable that facilities not only provide reliable operations management but also inform and influence the priorities of operations with data gleaned from a systematic marketing orientation.

In adopting a marketing research orientation, managers seek to make a consistent effort to understand customers' needs and expectations through formal/systematic/scientific means that verify or invalidate creative intuition. Creative intuition is informed through anecdotes, hunches, instinct, and random observations and can be dangerous when these subjective judgments remain untested or unchallenged.

Several concepts can combat the compliance mentality that develops in many organizations because of counterproductive financial reimbursement and regulatory environments. These concepts include management by fact, improved customer satisfaction, and cost savings—all aspects of QMI. Adaptation to vertical integration among different health care delivery organizations (ISNs or IDSs) is rapidly transforming the long-term care industry. These external issues of the industry or the marketplace force policy changes and process improvements that should benefit both residents and staff over the long term but cause major upheaval in facilities in the short term. By necessity, Woodland Care Center is adapting quickly to these new factors by introducing quality management principles, but the change in culture is not easy.

The difficulty of responding to shifting demands from the four customer groups (see Chapter 1) argues strongly for the implementation of QMI processes. QMI provides process control and measures trends and levels of data, thereby reducing risk and giving employees and managers the tools that allow flexible responses to altered requirements and expectations. Woodland's demographic data (see Chapter 3) illustrate these changes: Between Year 1 and Year 2, 50% of new admissions stayed less than 6 weeks (13.6% increase), and the average length of stay was 18.6 days (11.4% decrease). Furthermore, industry watchers predict accelerating changes.

Summary

Factors external to the long-term care facility are driving major changes in processes and policies within facility walls. Financial reimbursement systems influence, and often dominate, most health care decisions. Regulatory processes demand adherence to current minimal standards and may penalize continuous improvement attempts. Compliance therefore may lead to a status quo mentality; old quality assurance paradigms block quality improvement possibilities. To counteract these stresses, QMI offers a group of tools and techniques that provide practical, data-based decisions. By employing QMI tools and techniques, an organization also can guide decision making and minimize risk, thereby reducing the stress caused by rapid changes in the long-term care industry.

As people live longer, healthier lives, health care processes frequently are altered to match new requirements of all four customer groups: residents, families and designated caregivers, payer groups, and regulatory agencies. In this chapter the authors illustrated the changing industry environment and the marketplace and their impact on resident satisfaction, the long-term care industry, and QMI. Responsiveness to payer and regulatory groups (secondary customers of long-term care) and the impact of vertically integrated delivery systems and networks are forcing changes/improvements in both managers' and employees' daily work systems and expectations.

Will the long-term health care industry find these external industry transformations and the internal barriers and critical issues discussed in Chapter 4 to be acceptable challenges and opportunities, rather than overwhelming burdens? Woodland Care Center and its administrator are adopting quality management principles among the tools and techniques that will help them survive and thrive and continue their core mission of providing long-term health care for their resident population. Both internal and external customers are served more effectively when the savings and improved satisfaction ratings due to QMI may be applied to desired care processes instead of redoing tasks or wasting time, materials, and paperwork.

References

1   Stofac, T. (1994). Personal communication.

2   Booker, V. (1994). Personal communication.

3   Erickson, J.M. (1994, October). Personal communication.

4   Erickson, J.M. (1994). *Level A compliance decision making report.* Washington, DC: Foundation of the American College of Health Care Administrators.

5   Stofac, T. (1994). Personal communication.

6   Romano, M. (1994, November). Healthcare hookups. *Contemporary Long-Term Care, 32.*

7   Vanguard Group. (1994). Family research. *Sterling Review Report for Long-Term Care*, No. 1094, 2.

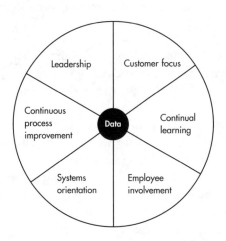

Chapter 6

MANAGEMENT BY FACT

DATA COLLECTION AND ANALYSIS ARE THE FOUNDATIONS OF DECISIONS

Previous chapters examined the need for transforming an organization's culture to encourage employee suggestions (and implement changes) and to require management to play an active role in quality management leadership. Implementation of these concepts leads to greater customer satisfaction, and they form the foundation of total quality management (TQM) and continuous improvement of processes and services. Improvements rest on a base of data collection and analysis, however, and data-based decision making is the focus of this chapter.

Application of the six core concepts of QMI enables organizations to turn data into usable information and allows long-term care facilities to implement management-by-fact methodologies. In other words, the results of number crunching determine whether processes should be changed and which processes have priority status. Successful QMI implementations typically include the following activities:

- Key quality indicators are established and monitored at regular intervals for core processes that operate across the facility.

- Individual departments track data that are compiled into a limited number of organization-wide indicators, in addition to tracking department-specific indicators.
- This data collection process allows the determination as to whether customer satisfaction measures and operational and clinical indicators have improved. These outcomes are the central criteria for success in the long-term care facility.
- The QMI data-based decision-making process is repeated again and again for continuing process improvement.
- After implementation, data are used to monitor and evaluate the success of the improvements made.

This chapter explains data collection and analysis methods that can be applied at a facility. These methods are illustrated with case study data gathered from Woodland Care Center and other facilities during their QMI implementation processes. The tools and techniques of QMI help managers to apply QMI concepts to the organization to measure process indicators and evaluate success. Appendix D supplements this chapter; it is a mini-handbook of potential QMI indicators and guidelines for data collection (also included is a brief synopsis of the key concepts of data collection and analysis to support QMI deployment efforts). QMI tools help managers prioritize among potential indicators to focus the measurement of both key organizational work systems and the processes and outcomes of those systems. The previous chapters have described common cause variation, the Plan–Do–Study–Act (PDSA) cycle, and other quality management data analysis techniques. These are necessary components of the QMI implementation process en route to letting data drive decision making—that is, management by fact. This chapter and Appendix D in particular focus on data collection and analysis tools and techniques as they underlie and support QMI processes.

Common Cause Analysis of Care Delivery Systems and Processes

(Note: Special cause and common cause variation of processes are examined in the remarks on p. 24 of Chapter 2; readers should review it before continuing. Keep in mind that if one particular problem requires frequent fire fighting, it is not a special cause; it is part of the everyday common cause system.)

Management by fact in long-term care requires knowledge of the actual common cause systems that produce long-term care services. Managers must consider which few among the many systems of support and service and which internal process factors are key predictors of success and determine process results for all of the individuals served by the organization.

Health care staff and physicians, regulatory agencies, and funding organizations typically define improvement in terms of the individual patient's diagnosis, prognosis, and clinical outcomes. They may not, however, recognize, identify, and track the common elements across all of their patients in common systems of care, record keeping, and communications. Like other organizations both inside and outside health care, Woodland's department staff seemed to fear that attention to overall common cause systems and processes would replace concern for the needs of individuals who are included in those processes. A thorough understanding of typical process behavior—the common cause system—protects the average individual from recurring problems. Collecting aggregate data or statistics on a facility's processes allows staff time to spend on truly unusual cases or significant problems that cut across systems and departments.

Uses of Data in QMI

Long-term care quality professionals, managers, team leaders, and team members collect QMI data for process improvement. Data are collected because they allow people to understand their work systems and to base their decisions on actual day-to-day process performance, as processes may or may not function as originally planned. Reasons to collect data and respond to the findings may include the following:

- To confirm the need for a process change
- To focus data collection efforts on core processes and key indicators
- To communicate the results of an investigation to the organization
- To measure results from subgroups or segments in order to compare their processes or outcomes (e.g., to compare floors/nursing units, weekends, shifts)
- To validate a decision to stop collecting data that are not useful
- To monitor previous process changes to ensure that the organization is "holding the gains"

Data help organizations decide which indicators to track, what actions to pursue, and which intervals to establish for measuring process change. The following case study provides a good illustration of data collection and analysis techniques.

Process Improvement in the Meal-Delivery Process
The effective use of several process improvement tools is illustrated at Harbor View Care Center, a facility that has decided to focus on processes in its short-term unit. This case study illustrates the use of several QMI tools: Pareto charts, flowcharts, checksheets, run charts, and cause-and-effect diagrams. It also demonstrates a cross-functional team at work, applying management by fact principles and using survey data effectively.

Residents of Harbor View Care Center were asked to complete a survey that measured their degree of satisfaction with a number of care and service areas. The survey results indicated that, in general, residents were happy with most aspects of care and service delivery; however, more than 40% of the residents surveyed were neutral, dissatisfied, or very dissatisfied with meal service. The quality council determined that these results were unacceptable and conducted one-to-one interviews with residents to determine the sources of dissatisfaction with the meal service. The council then created a Pareto chart (see p. 94) from the data to identify the most common sources of dissatisfaction.

Upon learning that the most frequent causes of resident dissatisfaction were "inappropriate food temperature" and "late delivery of food," the quality council decided to charter a process improvement team to study and improve the meal-delivery process. The team leader was the director of dietary services, and team members included two nursing assistants and two dietary aides representing day and evening shifts, a nurse, and a cook. Their project incorporated the PDSA pattern of process improvement.

Plan: The plan phase included understanding the current processes. As part of its improvement effort, the team constructed a flowchart, or process flow diagram, of the meal-delivery process (see p. 95).

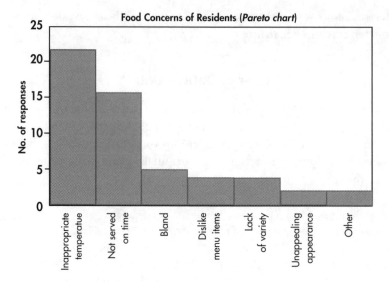

Do: After completing the flowchart, the team discovered an obvious delay in the process—the point at which a cart is filled and then placed in a holding area until the remaining carts are filled. Team members recognized that it made more sense to transport a cart to the nursing unit immediately after filling it. Because this step provided a quick and easy opportunity to reduce standing time and maintain constant food temperature, the director of dietary services implemented this change immediately. The team recognized, however, that other ways existed to improve this process but that these methods would require data collection and analysis.

A *checksheet* for data collection was developed, and staff collected data on meal cart delivery times for approximately 5 weeks. They measured the time from the point at which the first tray was placed on the meal cart to the time the last tray from the cart was delivered to residents. They plotted these data on a *run chart.*

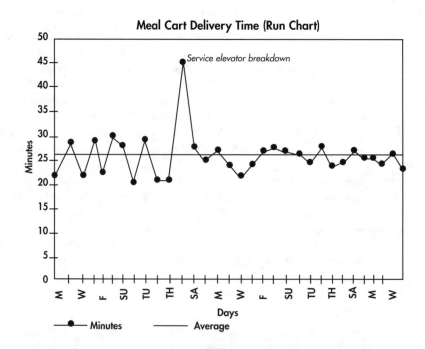

Tray Setup and Delivery Process Flowchart

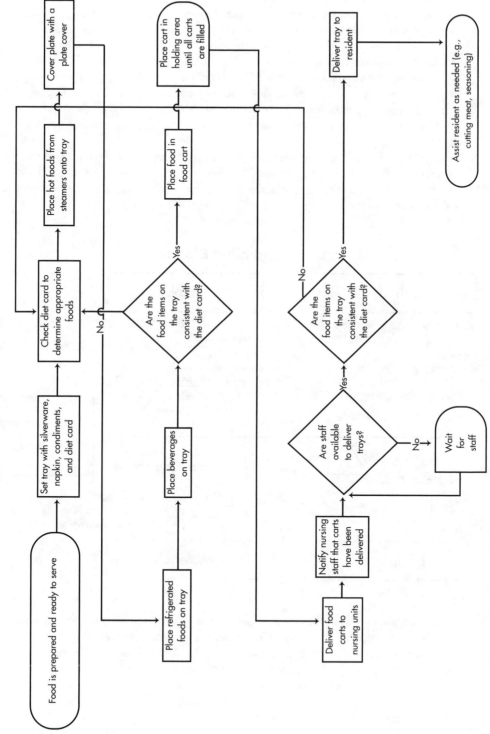

Study: In analyzing the run chart, staff discovered that their delivery process was often consistent, but all were surprised by an unusually large time span on the second Friday. Because this occurrence was so far out of the ordinary, they gathered data on this unusual pattern. Data identified the cause of this poor performance as a broken service elevator, which significantly delayed tray delivery. They recognized that this occurrence should be considered due to a *special cause variation.*

The elevator was repaired, and as the staff continued to collect data, they found the meal-delivery process to be quite stable. The run chart demonstrated only *common cause variation;* however, the team was not satisfied with the amount of variation that still existed in this process. The team wished to improve the average and to reduce the range between the highs and lows in staff performance.[1] Recognizing that the only way to reduce the common cause variation was to improve the capability of the process radically, the team set out to identify variables that were causing the variation. The team used a *cause-and-effect,* or "fishbone," *diagram* to identify all of the potential causes for delays in meal cart delivery.

Cause-and-Effect Diagram

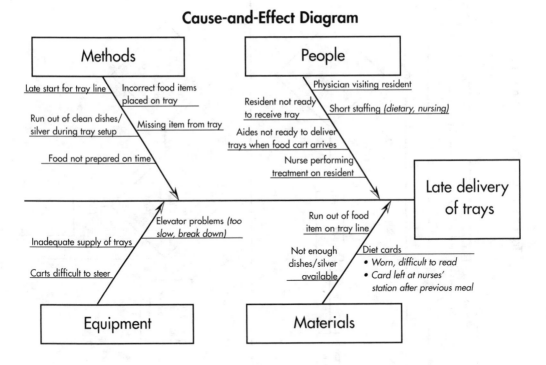

After brainstorming all of the possible reasons for delays in tray delivery, the team reached consensus based on intuition and experience. Team members identified three significant causes that, if improved, probably would make a significant reduction in variation and provide the greatest potential for reduction in tray delivery time:

1. Aides are not ready to deliver trays when cart arrives
2. Food items are incorrect; need to get new tray
3. Diet cards are worn and hard to read

Act: The team developed and implemented two improvement strategies that dramatically improved the meal service delivery:

1. Revise resident meal cards to identify the resident's diet, allergies, and food likes and dislikes clearly.
2. Dietary staff will call the nursing units before bringing the food cart to the unit, allowing nursing staff to prepare for tray delivery.

As the process improvement team continued to collect data and plot the data on the run chart, it noticed a downward shift in the center line (average), indicating a reduction in the tray-delivery time; the delivery times were much more predictable as well. Follow-up customer interviews with residents confirmed that, as a result of the improvement effort, they were now being served their meals on time. In addition, residents stated that the food temperature was more appropriate than before.

Continue to Improve and Monitor: The final phase of the PDSA cycle involved set-ting up periodic monitors at regular intervals to confirm that improvements have become permanent. The team selected several indicators, including data from periodic resident-satisfaction surveys.

The efforts of the process improvement team at Harbor View Care Center resulted in increased customer satisfaction, which was the primary goal. Before disbanding at the end of the improvement effort, the team spent its final meeting reviewing what had been learned. This review is called *reflective learning*. To the surprise of the team members, they discovered that they had learned a lot more than how to increase customer satis-faction:

*   The team realized that, although the problem-solving process took time, the methods used allowed it to find a solution that would last. The team was confi-dent that the improvements made would stand the test of time, unlike many of the previous "band-aid" or "fire fighting" solutions that often had been applied.
*   The team learned to use and apply several of QMI's most powerful tools and dis-covered how simple and effective they really are. The team used the PDSA cycle, Pareto charts, flowcharts, checksheets, run charts, and cause-and-effect diagrams.
*   The members also discovered the joy of working as a team. Everyone agreed that this project gave him or her an enormous appreciation for one another's work. One of the dietary aides stated, "I had no idea what nursing assistants and nurses really did until I had a chance to spend time with them on this team. I now under-stand why good communication between our departments is so important."
*   The director of dietary services (the team leader) was pleased. "Our project used the PDSA cycle to achieve such good results! We were able to go through a clas-sic 'management by fact' process. Now employees are pleased with the improve-ments, and customers are much more satisfied."

In the past the dietary and nursing departments were frequently at odds, pointing fingers and blaming one another when things did not run smoothly. As a result of the team's communicating with the rest of the nursing and dietary staff throughout the pro-ject, a new door was opened in the relationship between the departments.

Measuring Process Improvement

Organizations require data on the past behavior of systems to make decisions today and to reduce future risk. Actuarial data (statistics on group averages in different populations) en-able organizations to measure processes and outcomes—both levels and trends—to pre-dict the future behavior of these systems. Examples of data collection required for a full picture of long-term care processes might include

- Measures of process effectiveness, such as demographics, clinical outcomes, care delivery, psychosocial, and financial/operational data
- To encompass management by fact and QMI, the metrics (measurable indicators) also should include organizational issues such as staff turnover, management turnover, climate surveys, successful implementation of training, competitive and benchmark data, and others. Examples of other indicators are listed later in the chapter.
- All data selected should have a direct impact on customer satisfaction and resident outcomes, even when the metrics chosen involve internal organizational process efficiencies.
- The quality council should select several key processes that are part of the core systems and choose an indicator to track each process. The council should not be overly ambitious in trying to monitor too many processes. Individual departments may choose to monitor several additional indicators as well.
- Metrics that analyze efficient handoffs between different processes and departments are important. It is easy to overlook the "dead time" between steps in the process.
- Both percentage and number of occurrences may need to be tracked in order to compare performance. For example, if 50 residents have physical restraints, is that 50 out of 50 or 50 out of 350 total residents?
- Data collection and analysis, such as using run charts and Pareto charts, should target critical areas that are identified in the organization's mission or vision statements. The data should be used to set the organization's priorities.

Factors to consider in developing and deploying a data collection system include the following:

- What outcomes or process variables should be measured?
- Are the data already collected somewhere in the system? (Avoid duplicating efforts.)
- What data will be collected?
- How often will the data be collected?
- For how long will the data be collected?
- Will the potential data be sampled by collecting from a reduced portion of the total population, either at specified intervals or in a reduced quantity that is appropriately chosen?
- How will the data be collected?
- Who will collect the data?
- How will the data be used?
- Who will have access to the results?
- How will the data collection and analysis system be updated and improved over time?

Multifacility Data Comparisons

In multifacility organizations, some common factors should be tracked. An organization that is just beginning to implement QMI should select a few key process indicators from among its priority systems. They may be changed when priorities change, so the quality council must be realistic as to the number being tracked in the department or organization at any one time. Table 6-1 lists examples of potential indicators to be measured through time (these indicators also are appropriate for individual facilities).

To make the task of monitoring outcomes data reasonable and efficient yet thorough and comprehensive, a data analysis group can ensure that effective data collection systems

Table 6-1. Monitoring organizational outcomes

Senior management and the quality council will select a limited number of metrics that allow them to track key organization systems and provide advance warning of process changes. They may choose among indicators such as those that follow. The authors recommend that they be tracked on charts, which provide clear, straightforward warnings of process change.

Customer satisfaction measures
  Customer surveys and feedback systems
    (resident, family, physicians)
  Regulatory surveys: state and federal
  Complaint investigations

Clinical data
  Number of residents with physical restraints
  Number of residents receiving psychoactive
    drugs
  Number of residents with catheters
  Number of residents with pressure ulcers
    (stratify [subgroup] Stages 1–4)
  Rate of nosocomial infections
  Number of resident accidents/incidents

Operational data
  Number of admissions
  Number of transfers
  Number of discharges
  Number of deaths
  Admission sources
  Demographic data (e.g., gender, age of
    residents)

Human resources data
  Employee satisfaction surveys
  Turnover rate
  Number of open shifts per pay period
  Employee incident/accident rates
  Number of employees on workers' compen-
    sation
  Number of unemployment insurance claims
  Number of employee grievances
  Employee exit interviews
  Absenteeism rates
  Demographic data (e.g., gender, age of staff)

Financial data
  Census by payer type
  Medicare utilization
  Case mix
  Diagnosis and length of stay
  Accounts receivable
  Pool usage
  Therapy units
  Staff ratios per patient per day

are maintained and that the data collected are analyzed, summarized, and reported to the quality council and senior management.

These data should not be used to target or blame individuals' or facilities' performances. Senior leaders also should not use blame to control their middle managers. Instead, the council analyzes this information to identify patterns and trends and to prioritize organization-wide quality improvement initiatives. High performers may serve as benchmarks in the organization to guide process improvement elsewhere. One of the most difficult roles in QMI leadership is to model a nonblaming continuous improvement philosophy.

The need for actuarial/statistical data is particularly critical when working with managed care organizations. Future costs of health care can only be estimated when an organization calculates past costs and projects trends. Capitation methods for reimbursement are therefore based on average costs of health care per patient served per month or per day.

Segmentation and Aggregation of Data

Data analysis is most complete and provides the most understanding of process effectiveness when both the overall performance of a process (combined or aggregated data) and the performance of subgroups (segments) within that process are studied. Examples of aggregate and segmented data may include comparing a handful of clinical indicators (e.g., those in Table 6-1) both at the total organizational level (aggregate data) and the division or departmental level (segmented data). Both sets of data are needed for effective process or outcomes measurement. Segments of the total also may be compared against one another and against the average or median performance. Dividing the data in this way is called stratification or segmentation of the data population.

Graphs often provide a clear picture of differences between several segments of the population measured. For instance, if a manager were concerned about one segment of her population (e.g., one facility or one shift), she could compare it to the other segments on a line chart. She could study whether one facility or shift incurred more resident incidents (e.g., falls, accidents) than the other segments. Each of the facilities is one segment of the total; thus the organization could compare them (without blaming anyone) and could determine whether the individual subgroups matched the organization's overall, aggregated pattern. If they did not match, the quality council could try to learn how and why one segment and its process differ from the others. The groups often are displayed on graphs with one another or compared to the overall total to analyze why differences occur. It is important to look for the root causes of differences, not just the symptoms. This sort of process or segment comparison is one of the most important QMI activities for senior leaders and quality councils.

In marketing to different customer groups, segmented data are especially useful. The needs of each segment should be assessed separately. Process improvements are most effective when common priority issues are addressed together to minimize costs or enhance process consistency. In addition, the non-negotiable needs that may apply to one group but not another should be identified, and their needs may be compared with the organization's vision and strategic plans.

QMI Indicators to Track Clinical Effectiveness

Indispensable to either the fee-for-service or managed care payment schemes in a QMI environment is measuring the care process, particularly by establishing levels and trends of resident/family satisfaction. In addition to short-term satisfaction, however, the variables tracked also must analyze long-term clinical success. Such factors measure service outcomes and allow facilities to prioritize among processes those that need to be addressed by QMI tools and techniques. For example, one metric that can be used to gauge a resident's functional level and to track changes or improvement is the functional independence measure (FIM). FIM is the quantification of a complex cluster of factors. Other metrics that track changes in long-term clinical effectiveness are illustrated in the display on page 101. Examples of variables to track also may include infection rates, changes in condition, care plans, family support activities, and administrative or documentation processes. Several sets of psychosocial quality-of-life and clinical quality-of-care factors may be tracked for levels of performance and trends through time (see Appendix D).

Stofac[2] outlined a straightforward procedure for data collection: 1) gather information, 2) set standards (targets), and 3) track outcomes. QMI could not start more simply! The standards selected may reflect customer needs, desired clinical outcomes, regulatory

Clinical Data: Indicators that Track Process Outcomes

(Note: The department of nursing may choose to measure several indicators from this expanded list of clinical metrics. A quality council or leadership team in a multifacility setting also may track a handful of key outcome indicators (see Table 6-1) in order to compare departments or facilities on an ongoing basis.

Number of residents with physical restraints:
   Types of restraints:
Number of residents receiving psychoactive drugs/chemical restraints:
   Antipsychotics:
   Antianxiety/hypnotics:
   Antidepressants:
Number of residents on bowel and bladder retraining:
Number of residents receiving nutritional supplements:
Number of residents with pressure ulcers:
   Stage 1:
   Stage 2:
   Stage 3:
   Stage 4:
Rates of nosocomial infection:
Number of residents on antibiotics:
Number of resident accidents/incidents:
Number of residents receiving restorative nursing care:
   Ambulation:
   Dining:
Number of residents on behavior monitoring:
Number of residents receiving intravenous therapy:
Number of tracheotomies:
Number of residents receiving tube feeding:

compliance factors, or the reimbursement policies of payer groups. Tracking outcomes through time quantifies the levels of process performance and captures trends. Tracking process outcomes alerts staff to trends as they develop. (Department heads or other employees who complain that there is "no time for data collection" should consider the data collection guidelines in Appendix D, which encourage using existing data to minimize time expenditures.) Employees also may establish with management the thresholds of performance that trigger corrective action or other activity in response. For example, one facility's census committee becomes active only when the census drops below a certain numerical standard.

Keep in mind that a large number of data already are being collected for reporting purposes, either to the quality assurance committee or the regulatory and payer organizations. The QMI model, with its six core concepts, may provide ideas for sources of data, but managers must remember that both process measurements and outcomes/results should be analyzed. Quality assurance data are a small but very important piece of the data available to which managers must respond.

Anxiety in Managers and Employees

Often, frontline health care providers fear that collecting data across the entire organization depersonalizes and thereby inhibits the success of the care process. However, studying the common cause process of care allows residents to receive the best care more consistently. This is because what the typical process offers them each day on average is known to residents and care providers. Then, when a resident needs unusual attention that falls outside the everyday (common cause) system of processes, a decision may be made to provide for that individual's needs. This approach also minimizes overall costs.

Another fear also may inhibit employee participation in process measurement: Could QMI measurement uncover deficits in an employee's job performance? Management's active role before, during, and after implementation of QMI processes determines the levels of trust among the employee group. Careful, frequent communications about anticipated changes and active role modeling by senior executives are necessary. It is easy for old habits of blame and criticism to creep back into supervisors' and managers' speech and actions, and they should be on guard against these.

Key Outcomes and Key Process Indicators

Health care providers (e.g., nurses, physicians) may resist measurement of their own work process, as discussed in Chapter 4, but measuring patient outcomes is both acceptable and familiar in the industry. To control and improve the common cause process of health care, however, both the process that brings the end results and the outcomes must be measured to be sure that standards are met. Traditional quality assurance methods have focused on measuring quality outcomes. Outcomes are the results of a process. A QMI philosophy takes the data collection and analysis one step further by considering the process variables that can have an effect on the outcome. Outcomes indicators measure the effects that are caused by the ways in which the process behaves. Process indicators identify opportunities for improvement by pinpointing the causes (the process steps) that lead to the effects or results.

QMI efforts focus on looking "upstream" in the process to identify the key process variables, that is, those variables that have the greatest effect on the outcome. Improvement in how the process functions results in a more consistent and desirable outcome. Process measurements predict whether the results will be as planned. The following demonstrates several outcomes that can be measured (QA) and some process indicators that might be measured to ensure those outcomes:

Key outcomes	Key process indicators
"The food tastes good."	Prepared according to recipe
	Presented in an appealing way
	Food temperature
	Hot food served hot, cold food served cold
	Measured in actual degrees of temperature, in actual time sequence
"My paycheck is correct."	Time card completed accurately
	Deductions calculated correctly
	Inaccuracy measured in dollars/cents or in amount of time, if late

| "The wheelchair was repaired correctly and promptly." | Need for repair reported in a timely manner
Necessary tools available for repairs
Time measured between report of need for repair and pickup, repair, delivery |

All of the key process variables are quantifiable. Note, however, that some of the measures call for a *count* of the number of occurrences, and some call for *measurable* data such as time, temperature, or dollars. We recommend the collection of *measurable* data whenever possible because they tell more about the factor being measured than can a simple count or yes-or-no answer. Measurable data provide a better investigative tool to uncover root causes (process steps) that lead to problems. Following are two examples of count versus measurable data:

Food temperature: The variance in degrees from the desired temperature is measurable data and may be tracked on run charts. A simple yes-or-no count may be tracked, but these charts supply less information about the food-delivery process. More information is needed about the "yes" or "no" responses to identify the causes for process problems.

Time card accuracy or deductions: Yes-or-no counts measure freedom from errors. Variations in dollars or minutes, however, provide more information about the depth of the problem and its frequency. Measurable data, particularly when displayed on run/trend charts, encourage study of the root causes for process behavior.

A Measure of Management

One area of data collection that is often overlooked is measuring the success of the management process itself. A fundamental concept of QMI is that continuous process improvement requires data on which to base decisions about change. Managers may consider measuring the success of their own management style with an employee survey or may track turnaround time on decision making or paperwork. Management processes are no less measurable or in need of improvement than other employees' work efforts, and the effectiveness of management support often determines the success of other employees' outcomes. QMI requires management by fact on the part of the complete organization, that is, the use of long-term data for decision making for managers as well as employees.

Computer-Based Information Systems

Computer systems that promise to help control process quality and improve process outcomes are developing quickly in long-term care. Computers often are required to track data for regulatory and payer evaluations of care processes as well as for internal monitoring of care processes. (See the section on the prospective payment system in Chapter 5.) Few systems, however, have evolved much beyond automating paper-based systems that tracked individual residents' care. A good computerized system for integrating quality management should provide data totals and averages in both subgroups of residents and the total population, comparisons of levels and trends through time on graphs, and frequent automatic generation of summary statistics across the facility, as well as through a multifacility organization. Some reports also are prepared for boards of trustees. Unlike data that report only the status and care pathways for residents, these statistics describe a facility's common cause systems and allow staff at all levels to agree on priorities for improvement. These data answer the following types of questions:

- Which process should we address first?
- Which processes should take top priority in our time and efforts?
- How can we satisfy increasing customer expectations and anticipate their needs?
- Where can we reduce costs best in terms of setup, waste, and rework?

More sophisticated computer packages generate automatic reports, compiling or aggregating the data from many departments to provide overall systems–level statistics for senior management and the quality council's planning and tracking purposes. Many organizations open up much of their database to all of their employees, demonstrating true employee involvement; team leaders and members are proud when they see proof of their effective problem–solving efforts. Some reports and indicators also are used in establishing a vision and in strategic planning by the board of directors. (Juran's quality trilogy from Chapter 2 comes to mind: The data provide necessary information for quality planning, quality control, and quality improvement at all levels of the organization.) Using data that already are being collected for QA and regulatory reports reduces data collection costs. A discussion of using Minimum Data Set (MDS) data in this way follows; data drive quality improvement, quality reporting, and QA.

Quality Indicators Focus Process Management/Quality Improvement Efforts

The Center for Health Systems Research and Analysis (CHSRA) at the University of Wisconsin, Madison, under the direction of Dr. David Zimmerman, has created a long-term care quality indicator system. This project, funded by the Health Care Financing Administration (HCFA), gives providers a tool that assists in objectively measuring quality in their facilities, as well as enabling data comparisons with peers. It turns MDS data, which all long-term care facilities already collect, into information. The CHSRA system also allows providers to demonstrate their quality of care to consumers and purchasers of care. The system measures 12 quality indicator domains. Each domain contains measurable indicators that measure either processes or outcomes. A process indicator reflects a course of action taken by the facility in response to the assessed needs of a resident. An outcome indicator reflects the status of a resident in terms of functional ability or clinical condition. The system allows for risk adjustment; that is, some of the indicators separate resident populations into high-risk and low-risk groups. The 12 indicator domains are

1. Accidents
2. Clinical management
3. Elimination/continence
4. Nutrition/eating
5. Psychotropic drug use
6. Sensory functioning/communication
7. Behavioral/emotional patterns
8. Cognitive patterns
9. Infection control
10. Physical functioning

11. Quality of life
12. Skin care

As an example, the skin care domain measures the prevalence of Stages 1–4 pressure ulcers. The number of residents with pressure ulcers in the most recent assessment is divided by the total number of residents. Each indicator can be defined at the individual resident level (e.g., whether the resident has a pressure ulcer) and the facility level (e.g., proportion of residents with pressure ulcers). Facilities are provided with facility/resident-level quality improvement reports, protocols for determining problems, general quality improvement guidelines, and quality improvement–specific technical assistance tools.

This type of automated, computer-based system provides the long-term care facility with a means to measure objectively the quality of resident care and to improve resident satisfaction. As a quality improvement tool, MDS results also help focus improvement efforts only in areas that really need them, saving resources and money.

Customer Data Required for Decisions on Process Improvement

All decisions about process improvement should be made with consideration of the benefits to customers. Ultimately, all such decisions affect external customers (residents, family members, payers, regulators; see also Chapter 1), even when the initial purpose is to benefit customers who are internal to the organization, that is, fellow employees.

Jablonski defines internal customers as those individuals and departments inside the organization who use output from or are the beneficiaries of other departments' tasks and activities. They perform tasks, provide technical services, and use the resources of the organization to enable it to meet the needs of external customers.

> Many efficiency and customer satisfaction problems can be traced to conflicting needs of internal and external customers. In many cases, healthcare processes are designed to meet the needs of internal customers. . . . A balance must be struck [between needs of both internal employees and the four groups of external customers]. . . . Quality improvement efforts that make this distinction and plan changes accordingly are more apt to succeed than those that focus solely [either] on the needs of external customers or on internal efficiency.
>
> Customer needs and expectations should serve to drive development of new service offerings. . . . Improvement efforts that do not identify customer satisfaction as their primary objective fail the basic litmus test of quality. . . . <u>Regardless of the level of effort expended, the elegance of the testing and reporting mechanisms, and the degree of employee involvement, if the customer's expectations are not met the effort has been wasted.</u>[3]

Data Collected During the Woodland Care Center Project: Methods, Results, and Evaluations

QMI Surveys

Evaluations of Woodland's senior staff measured their acceptance of QMI concepts at both the start and finish of the project. Respondents wrote answers to six questions. The survey and summary of responses are found in Appendix E, and the data are discussed in Chapter 3. Aggregated results of the preassessments spotlighted the senior staff's concerns and assumptions about quality management issues for use in subsequent planning sessions and discussions, such as department head meetings. No impression was gained of bias or distortion in senior staff responses, and people seemed willing to take part in both surveys.

Survey assessments should be repeated periodically to study shifts in attitudes and ratings. An assessment of employees' attitudes through surveying only a sample (subgroup) or through discussions in focus groups also may aid in strategic quality planning for the quality council and the communications team. Reporting the results of such assessments often promotes buy-in by employee groups and serves as a "preview of coming events."

Data Used in Department Quality Improvement Projects

Woodland's department heads each chose one project to complete. These projects were successful and generated a sense of satisfaction when they were completed. As discussed in Chapter 3, however, only 5 of the 15 projects included data collection or data analysis before decisions were made on solutions, despite some preliminary planning and encouragement from both the facility's consultant and the administrator. This reluctance to use data for decision making is very common at first. The following Woodland projects included data collection:

- Therapeutic Recreation: Reduced time folding and preparing newsletter; will include survey of readership interests in future issue to allow data to determine future newsletter contents
- Occupational Therapy: Concerned with interruptions during morning appointments with residents; data before/after showed reduction in number of telephone calls and pages
- Nutritional Services and Speech-Language Therapy (joint): Improved quality and appearance of thickened liquids; preparation time was measured and reduced; survey was prepared for staff and resident reactions to validate success of process changes
- Maintenance: Monitored the temperature of warm water in all of the rooms
- Business Office: Tracked timesheets and errors in paychecks; analyzed causes of handwritten checks to reduce clerical time

Staff believed that the quality improvement projects were worthwhile, and several staff members requested another project immediately. Projects also opened some beneficial joint problem solving between departments. The administrator intends that the next series of projects to be chosen will include one or more measurable variables and simple formal data analysis, preferably including graphs. As QMI tools, graphs provide clear data analysis of process changes through time and effectively gain support for joint projects or for other process improvement efforts. Graphs and charts are examined further in the display on pages 107–109.

Use of Survey Data

Surveys provide a straightforward means of gathering information on customers' or employees' opinions and desires. Survey data analysis may be very simple or highly statistical. Survey results are powerful spotlights on possible areas for improvement, even when the surveys are not sophisticated. Results may not be precise because of sample size or bias introduced by survey construction or question content. Still, respondents appreciate being asked about their beliefs and processes and usually provide valuable information that helps administration, nursing staff, or other departments set priorities for integrating quality management. (A brief discussion of working with survey results is included in Appendix D.)

Employee and Customer Satisfaction Surveys

The understanding that results from simple totals, averages, and percentages may increase the level of comprehension regarding both employees' and customers' needs or attitudes in a QMI environment. Like other process data, changes in levels and trends should be tracked through time to alert managers to possible shifts or other changes in employee attitudes or designated process areas. Similarly, customer processes and outcomes must be measured and tracked through time. Surveys allow the quantification and prioritization of people's opinions. Survey results may then be used to affect employee satisfaction and retention or customer care and service processes.

Survey Response

It is essential that management respond to issues raised by surveys, or they waste time and increase cynicism on the part of their respondents. For example, Woodland's QMI survey results were used to shape its QMI projects, and handouts to department heads reported survey outcomes (see Appendix E). Management or other surveyors must follow through in response to the gathered data. The quality, seriousness, and timeliness of response affect future attitudes toward similar survey requests. The results should be summarized for respondents, including family members, when the analysis is completed.

Using Charts to Analyze Data and Communicate Results

The two most powerful QMI measurement tools are familiar; they are simple to understand and to construct. Pareto diagrams and run charts (also called trend charts) were used by Harbor View's senior staff and individual departments for strategic planning and process improvement. This display contains a brief synopsis of the charts' construction.

Pareto Diagram

The Pareto diagram is a bar graph that shows the frequency of the events or categories being studied. The bars are placed in descending order from left to right. This placement allows the organization to assign each of the occurrences to a category and then focus on those categories that occur the most frequently and are the most important.

Pareto ranking is an effective decision-making device for all types of data, including surveys, because it draws attention to the category that may have the highest reward for a facility's continuous improvement efforts. For example, the results of Woodland's QMI surveys were included in Chapter 4, in comparison with the results that were reported in the literature and by top- and middle-level health care managers. To help Woodland set priorities among its QMI survey responses, barriers identified by department heads were ranked in Pareto order, placing issues that received the most consensus at the top. These data appear in Appendix E.

Harbor View collects and analyzes data for both strategic planning and decision-making purposes. In an employee satisfaction survey employees identified seven factors in response to the question, "What factors are most important for your job satisfaction?" The data were collected from a group of 205 employees and placed into seven categories. The categories of respectful supervision and education/training are shown to be the "vital few." "Vital few" describes the few most important factors to be studied, in contrast to the many other possible improvements, which often are called the "useful many." It is useful to address these issues, but more productive results are found in the "vital few."

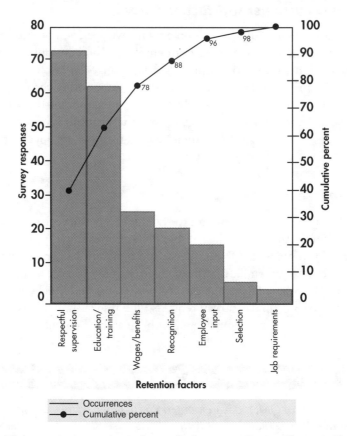

An optional line graph may appear above the bars on a Pareto diagram. This line traces the cumulative percent of the seven categories, as they accumulate from left to right, and is helpful in pinpointing where the vital few end and the useful many begin.

Run Chart or Line Chart

A run chart is a graph in which the single item being measured is plotted to show the levels of performance through time. Once data have been collected, the data points are placed on the graph chronologically. When the average or "centerline" is added, a process improvement team is able to interpret stability of the process. For example, nonrandom patterns in the variation, shifts in the process, or an upward or downward trend in the data may indicate the presence of special causes or upcoming process problems. A run chart also allows the team to analyze the performance of a process compared with baseline data and to monitor actions that have been taken to improve performance. In addition, it is a valuable tool in assessing how capable a process is of meeting established standards.

Individual departments at Harbor View use data to track their performance. For example, the recreation therapy department offered current events activities to residents. The activities director wanted to gauge how many residents on average attended the events and whether specific types of activities drew more participants. Based on attendance, the activities director could monitor customer satisfaction and plan further improvements.

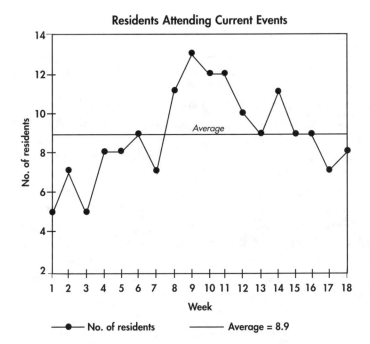

Residents Attending Current Events

According to the run chart attendance was down toward the end of the survey period, but in order to be certain that the information is correct, the activities director must collect several more data points. (*Note:* Traditionally, statisticians look for 7 data points in a row, or at least 9 of 11 data points in an upward or downward direction for a trend, or 11 of 13 data points ascending or descending.)

A warning contained in the professional literature and voiced by experienced long-term care quality managers regarding uses of survey data is repeated here: *Customer satisfaction should be tied to long-term clinical improvement or rehabilitation, not to short-term feelings of family or employee satisfaction. (For residents who are dying or have an ongoing health condition and who cannot be rehabilitated, look for a slowing pace of deterioration, which indicates clinical progress.) In other words, the clinical aspects of care should be the drivers of process improvement rather than marketing initiatives or improved scores on survey forms.*

Family Satisfaction Surveys

The measurement of customer satisfaction and identification of customer needs are key to the success of any QMI project. As in all nursing facilities, although resident satisfaction is the primary focus of all customer groups, the four customer groups differ in their needs and should be studied separately. Long-term care facilities often choose to interview residents because many of them are unable to respond to standard pen-and-paper surveys on their own. Facilities also may gather information through a sample group of residents or through focus groups.

Because many residents of long-term care facilities are frail and may be unable to make decisions, their surrogates (i.e., family members/caregivers) often are surveyed in their place. These surrogates should express their own needs, however, as well as attempt to communicate the needs of the residents. Several articles in the professional literature have shown statistically that families' responses do not reflect residents' attitudes with accuracy. In other words, the family/caregiver customer group should be surveyed regarding its own needs, with somewhat less emphasis placed on their response as surrogates for residents. A sample family satisfaction survey is contained in Appendix F. A statistical analysis of the results of a somewhat more sophisticated survey conducted at Abbey View Nursing Home, a sister facility of Woodland Care Center, follows.

The external consultant who was active at Woodland Care Center also was a member of the Abbey View Nursing Home survey team. In the Abbey View survey of family satisfaction there were statistical treatments of survey data, such as simple linear regression, multiple regression, and other statistical tests. Abbey View's findings were reported to Abbey View's administrator to provide quantitative bases for process improvement decisions. Like Woodland, three levels of nursing care are provided at Abbey View, depending on length of stay and acuity of care required. Abbey View's family satisfaction survey showed no significant differences among the three floors in their levels of customer satisfaction, however. (Other factors considered statistically included groupings by age, sex, and length of stay of resident.)

The 26 variables included on the survey were grouped into six areas: overall satisfaction, care and therapy, food, facility, activities, and administration. Through statistical analysis (multiple regression), the process improvement team showed that the best predictors of family satisfaction included five component factors: 1) quality of nursing care, 2) quality of care given by nursing assistants, 3) provision of privacy and dignity, 4) quality of the air, and 5) promptness of information regarding resident's condition. In fact, it was statistically shown that of the 26 variables surveyed, these five factors explained 66.4% of families' total satisfaction. Four of the five factors fall into the care and therapy (i.e., interpersonal) area of the survey and are within the control of the facility and the staff. Studies in the professional literature confirm that the quality of the interpersonal relationships among the staff and the residents and their family members/caregivers has the most impact on customer satisfaction.[4]

Several findings from the Abbey View survey are of interest to facilities that will use family satisfaction surveys:

- The three floor units were not statistically different based on their care levels (e.g., Alzheimer's, subacute), although the team had anticipated they might be.
- "Overall satisfaction" averaged 4.2 out of a possible 5 and "Abbey View met my expectations" averaged 4.1, both of which were slightly better than "good" ratings.
- Complaints that were voiced in the open-ended comments (qualitative data) were similar to those reported by other facilities and to reports in the literature. Their tone seemed helpful rather than highly critical.

Customer dissatisfaction factors chiefly included areas of concern in the care and therapy section of the questionnaire, thus implying that interpersonal issues (e.g., personal appearance and care of the resident, relationships with nursing assistants, prompt and accurate information, and quality of care delivered by nurses) are the central concerns of most families/caregivers. Staff may want to focus their attention in this area to effect the greatest impact on family/caregiver satisfaction. Facility issues (e.g., odors, security, safety, cleanliness) were the second most important category to this group.

The implications for improving customer satisfaction at Abbey View, at Woodland Care Center, and in the long-term care industry are clear: Abbey View, Woodland Care Center, and other long-term care facilities should focus family satisfaction efforts on interpersonal relationships in order to optimize their outcomes.

Process Factors to Track QMI Implementation

Finison[5] provided guidelines specific to the QMI environment in his discussion on selecting variables for measurement that provide worthwhile, timely results. His "good health care measurements" were derived by the Health Care Committee, Quality Management Division, of the American Society for Quality (ASQ). (See Appendix J for details on this professional quality management organization.) Consider the following in choosing quality measures:

1. Select measures that line staff can collect and chart efficiently.
2. Position measures to reflect continuous quality improvement (i.e., do not place any arbitrary boundaries on the measures).
3. Measures should be made available to line staff.
4. Measures should align key customer demands with the processes that produce these customer outcomes.
5. The selected measures should produce data in which the organization has a genuine interest.
6. Variables (continuous data) should be chosen over attributes data (yes/no) as the former are more statistically powerful.

Finison's article also provided health care applications and illustrations of these eight metrics. Appendix D contains several other lists of possible metrics for clinical (quality of care) and psychosocial (quality of life) data.

It may be helpful for departments, teams, and the quality council to use a common format (Figure 6-1) to define and compare their selected indicators. For example, after priorities have been set by using the multifunctional systems orientation matrix (Table 4-1), the descriptors in the indicator description matrix ensure that the process and the problem have been clearly defined and targeted.

Future Prospects

As integrated delivery systems multiply over the next few years, demographics for the resident populations of nursing facilities such as Abbey View, Harbor View, or Woodland Care Center will continue to change. Units that offer subacute, short-term care, in particular, will require more timely data collection and measurements to allow a prompt response to documentation and reporting requirements. Woodland's population demographics reflect managed care policies that emphasize short-term care and rehabilitation, with many stays lasting from several days to 6 weeks, as detailed earlier in Woodland's data. Administration and clinical policies will require flexibility, consistency, and efficiency to meet these chang-

---

Indicator Selection Record

Desired change or outcome:

Problems or barriers to the change:

Activities to address the problem:

Indicator(s) selected to measure progress:

Measurement interval:

Target dates for anticipated change (Optional—Target Goals):

Figure 6-1. The indicator selection record helps to ensure that organizational priorities, strategies, and policies guide data collection and analysis efforts and helps management deploy the quality council's priorities into the individual departments. It ensures that teams and managers are in agreement as to how to "cascade" the organizational priorities down through the systems into daily work, which aligns department efforts with organizational systems improvement priorities. The characteristics for any chosen QMI indicator, outlined above, should be easily described. Department heads or managers may want to keep a notebook or file of current indicators for their department or across the organization.

ing customer needs. Organizations will control risk by tracking key indicators through time. Using QMI, improved data analysis will allow effective responses to these trends.

Summary

Many discussions in the long-term care industry in the 1990s revolved around competing systems to guide integration of quality management activities and processes in daily work. The key to long-term success, however, is that the selected activities include data-based decisions as well as a cultural transformation. Examples of successful data-based activities include the following:

- Establishing threshold levels to trigger action
- Benchmarking to study best practices and best performers elsewhere
- Establishing goals and targets as desired outcomes
- Tracking trend direction and improvement rates on charts to monitor and guide process improvement efforts
- Using data not only to improve processes but to completely reengineer them
- Performing other quantified decision making processes

However it is implemented, QMI results in impressive gains in resident and employee satisfaction and reductions in costs of quality. Process improvements ensure reliable, timely process outcomes for long-term care facilities and their staffs and residents. These results depend, however, on a number of basic requirements:

- An understanding on the part of administration and staff of the power of management by fact
- A willingness to practice effective data collection and analysis techniques to turn data into usable information
- A good foundation in the basic QMI tools and techniques, including an acceptance (by both management and staff) of the active role of employees in process change and service improvement
- Priorities established for QMI efforts to focus staff and management attention and to allocate expenditure of scarce resources
- Ongoing monitoring of key process indicators at regular intervals
- Data-based decision making at all levels of the organization
- An emphasis on long-term clinical outcomes for the resident, which are measured through time
- A nonblaming attitude on the part of managers and senior executives—departments or facilities demonstrating consistently high performance may serve as benchmarks in the group; low performers should not be "blamed," however, because they probably perform well when other measures are used

By using data effectively and employing management by fact techniques, the "transformation" of the organization (Deming's term) is ensured. The core concepts of QMI, the 3-phase quality management integration process, and the PDSA cycle assist in implementing QMI processes. Effective work processes and increased customer satisfaction are the rewards.

References

1   A control chart (what we call "a run chart that went to college") would be much more accurate in calculating whether this process is statistically significant. A control chart is among the classic tools that are used in statistical process control. Unfortunately, this chart requires much more detailed explanation than is possible within this book.

2   Stofac, T.J. (1994). *Continuous quality initiatives: A manager's guide* (p. 73). Des Moines, IA: Briggs Corporation.

3   Jablonski, R. (1992, November). Customer focus: The cornerstone of quality management. *Healthcare Financial Management,* 17–18. (Emphasis added)

4   Fisk, T.A., Brown, C.J., Cannizzaro, K.G., & Naftal, B. (1990, June). Creating patient satisfaction and loyalty. *Journal of Health Care Marketing, 10,* 5–15.

5   Finison, L.J. (1992, April). What are good health care measurements? *Quality Progress,* 41–42.

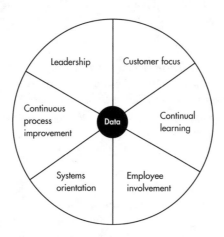

Chapter 7

PATHWAY TO SUCCESS

STRATEGIC APPROACHES TO IMPLEMENTING QMI

The young nursing assistant from Chapter 1 left her facility when she felt that she was not being supported by the director of nursing or the administration's policies. To that facility, she became just another data point on its "turnover" trend chart. She felt lucky to be hired at Carver Health Care Center—and they were fortunate to recruit and retain her.

My job as a nursing assistant has really changed over the past year here at Carver Health Care Center. It all began when we started hearing a lot of talk about "quality management integration (QMI)." At first I didn't give it much thought. They've started a lot of different programs at this facility in the past, but the programs always went away. This time, things really have changed.

We went through training in a lot of different kinds of areas—customer service, data collection and analysis, process improvement—and then I was asked to serve on a process improvement team that was charged with improving the admissions process. It used to be just the department heads who would work on this kind of stuff. But our administrator told us that to make this facility the best it could be, we all would have to be involved.

I liked being a part of the admissions team. There were people from dietary, housekeeping, and social services on the team who I didn't know very well when we started, but by the time we got done, we were really a team. When I made suggestions, my input was valued and used. It felt good to know that I was a part of making something work better.

There were a lot of new things that I've learned how to do. I learned how to flow-chart a process. I learned what other departments do, and I see how what I do fits in with what they do. I learned how to collect data and use them to monitor our progress. We actually decreased the time it took to do an admission, and we became a lot more organized.

I have a friend who is thinking about becoming a nursing assistant. I told her she should apply at my facility. I work really hard at what I do, but it's worth it because I know that my work is appreciated.

Life is also different for managers in facilities that have implemented QMI processes and values. One of the most challenging leadership positions in a long-term care organization is the director of nursing, the individual who oversees the great majority of frontline care providers, monitors their quality standards, and ensures the residents' clinical and psychosocial satisfaction. The director of nursing featured in Chapter 1 who was so frustrated by her job, her employees, and the regulatory environment relaxed once QMI was implemented.

I never thought I could enjoy my work as much as I do now. Oh, sure, there are still days that get pretty hectic as the director of nursing, but it's different from the way it used to be. Our facility has made a significant turnaround since we've adopted QMI principles. After I went through several sessions of quality management training, I began applying what I learned to my department. I started two quality improvement teams to work on the bath-scheduling process and the order transcription process. In the past I would have just made the changes that I thought were needed. Now, instead of me doing all the work and then telling people how it was going to be, the people who actually work within the process are making it much better than I ever could alone. I've learned how to share responsibility with my staff, and I trust them to make good decisions. With the QMI data that we routinely collect, my staff and I are able to detect patterns and trends and to pick up on potential problems before they get out of hand. This allows us to be proactive instead of reactive to symptoms of problems.

The biggest change I've noticed is with the nursing assistants. They are part of the QMI process of collecting data and then using the data to make decisions. For example, they started collecting data on how long it took for call lights to be answered. They reviewed the data and came up with a plan for a call light–answering system that included all staff working on a particular wing. They continued collecting data using this new system and found that they cut the call light–answering time by 50%! The nursing assistants were thrilled, but our residents were even happier. QMI has helped increase our employee retention rate, too.

Our facility is not just your average nursing home anymore. Both the resident and employee satisfaction surveys continue to show improvement each time we do them. I really love working here now.

When we began constructing the concept of QMI implementation in long-term care, we felt the need for a model that would draw together the quality management principles that have been applied in many other industries with great success. The six core QMI concepts and their reliance on data should be considered whenever making process improvements is proposed. The six core concepts of QMI and their reliance on data appear in the QMI model at the beginning of this book; the guidelines for implementing each QMI concept are discussed in Chapter 1.

In our description of QMI, we addressed issues of central importance to administrators, quality directors, and managers. The following bulleted items detail some of the issues we encourage managers and their staff to consider as the quality journey is begun.

- Begin by developing an understanding of the concepts and history of TQM and CQI in business and industry and, more specifically, in the long-term care industry. This knowledge provides an overall picture of the philosophy and a solid foundation on which to build.
- The long-term care industry emphasizes restorative health programs and a person's return to a noninstitutional setting when possible. In addition, integrated delivery systems (IDSs) that network a variety of health care services are radically and swiftly changing the expectations of health care professionals, as well as those of residents and family members. These industry changes make an understanding of QMI tools and techniques vital because these techniques provide timely information or warning signals of change.
- Long-term care managers need to have a common understanding of
  - Who their customers are (the four customer groups: residents, families, payer groups, and regulatory agencies)
  - What their customers' expectations are (recognizing that expectations and requirements can evolve rapidly over time)
  - Management's role in implementing QMI
  - The principles of data collection and analysis and management by fact
  Managers also must understand the flexibility that is required to manage in a quality management environment.
- Determine and plan how to introduce quality management philosophy and processes within the facility or organization. The 3-phase quality management integration process described in Chapter 3 is a framework that has proved useful at Woodland Care Center and many other organizations. The plan should include
  - Establishment of an infrastructure that supports the quality initiatives (e.g., a quality council, process improvement teams)
  - Training senior staff and supervisors
  - Development of strategic quality plans
  - Implementation of quality improvement projects that are supported by the quality council and facilitated by trained facilitators or other leaders
  - Development of a method to measure the facility's progress
- Recognize the barriers and critical issues, both internal and external to the long-term care facility, that may affect the success of QMI implementation. Apply the overview of barriers and critical issues in Chapters 4 and 5 to strengthen the organization's transformation.
- Data collection and analysis must become a way of life for long-term care staff and management. The measurement of quality outcomes and the process variables that influence results allow staff to determine what processes and systems need to be improved and how to improve them. Through QMI, risk can be limited, cost-effective services can be provided, customer satisfaction can be measured, and the success of residents' long-term care outcomes can be analyzed.
- As the organization develops within the managed care environment of the 21st century, it will be important for the management team to recognize how the QMI tools of data collection and analysis enable the long-term care facility to manage its processes and systems better. Managers must remember that key processes interrelate within the most important organization-wide systems. Recognizing interdepartmental linkages is a key principle in

QMI, breaking down many old assumptions of budgeting and traditional department/ organization leadership. Maintaining a systems orientation is a particular focus of management and the quality council.

New Roles for Management and Employees Following QMI Implementation

The way the management treats the staff is the way the staff treats the residents.
William Thomas, M.D., founder of the Eden Alternative

Most of the issues discussed in this book, including the barriers considered in Chapter 4, are management issues, under management control. Management teams should identify and remove those barriers to enable employees to work on process improvements unencumbered. This is true employee empowerment. Management's leadership role is the foundation of QMI success. QMI responsibility and leadership cannot be delegated down into the organization.

Following the implementation of QMI concepts, skilled, knowledgeable, and involved employees gain flexibility. They can then respond more effectively to a quickly changing health care environment, regulations, and customer expectations. This is the power of participative management, a partnership of employees and management to jointly benefit their customers. QMI also strengthens the facility's process stability so that it can avoid large fines because of deficiencies during the survey process.

Participative management principles guide the interactions of management and employees, with a cascading impact on the interpersonal relationships of staff with residents. As management cares for its employees, management's internal customers, so the employees care for the residents, the external customers who determine a facility's success. These strategic decisions are leadership issues and underlie all QMI and employee involvement efforts.

Working with Internal and External Quality Consultants

Organizations may decide to provide internal support, hire an external consultant, or decide to work in collaboration with both. Woodland Care Center elected to work with an external consultant during their QMI start-up phase. In your strategic planning, provide for additional training and planning time if the facility's administrator and quality director intend to proceed without support from an outside professional. Different learning curves must be anticipated in such a case. Building internal capabilities in this way takes longer, but it provides lasting benefits for the organization. The roles of internal and external consultants may be compared as follows.

Many organizations choose to provide quality management support from a person who is dedicated solely to QMI as a "consultant." This person may be a full-time employee (internal consultant) or a person hired for that project from outside (external consultant). Typically, the external consultant brings a breadth of knowledge from outside the organization, whereas the internal consultant develops a depth of knowledge of the specific facility or multifacility operation. Providing a consultant may signal the board's or administration's intent to proceed with QMI. A multifacility organization frequently chooses the internal consultant, often placing one at the corporate level as well as others in individual facilities. Budget considerations, corporate culture, and strategic planning often determine which course to follow. (Successful organizations may choose not to have dedicated QMI support at all. In this case the quality infrastructure—administrator, quality council, board of directors—must ensure that the policies and activities of QMI are implemented. This, in itself, can become a full-time job.)

The benefits of providing focused QMI support from an internal or external consultant include having a knowledgeable individual who is available for full-time training, solving problems, or facilitating teams; a person with oversight responsibility, accountable for shepherding the process; and an on-site QMI professional. The quality consultant's role encompasses facilitating the establishment of customer satisfaction policies and the development of a QMI philosophy and vision. The QMI professional engages in process planning and integration and assists in designing the QMI structure and systems.

Establishing Customer Satisfaction

Knowledge of customer needs and expectations forms the foundation of the quality management process. The quality consultant provides support in conducting customer needs analysis to identify expectations and assists programs/departments in determining effective measures to gauge customer satisfaction. He or she assists in establishing customer satisfaction feedback mechanisms and promotes the use of data measurement and analysis of internal and external customer satisfaction.

Developing a QMI Philosophy and Vision

The quality consultant is responsible for working with senior leaders to establish a QMI philosophy and vision that is consistent with the mission and values of the organization. From this work, the quality consultant facilitates implementation and maintenance of the quality management process. The QMI process should be designed to enhance productivity within the organization as well as with partners such as external suppliers and subcontractors. A quality consultant seeks opportunities to communicate the organization's quality management philosophy to both internal and external constituents. Consultants work with all levels of facilities to integrate the philosophy into day-to-day operations.

Recognizing that initiating a quality management philosophy requires organizational transformation, the consultant serves as an organizational change agent. Consultants help to create an open, problem-solving climate throughout the organization, in which problems are confronted and differences are clarified both within and between groups. Consultants facilitate planned change based on the organization's mission, vision, values, and strategic plan.

Acting as Organizational Change Agent

A quality consultant assesses the organizational culture to identify its current state, assists management in defining a desired future situation, and facilitates strategic planning to reach the desired objectives. A consultant demonstrates a strong belief in the importance of quality and acts as a role model for desired quality competencies. Quality consultants persist in the transition process toward quality management despite potential resistance from others. As change often produces varying degrees of resistance, they support the facility's staff through the stress of organizational transition and assist in reducing resistance to change.

In general, the quality consultant uses a collaborative consulting model to establish a supportive relationship designed to broaden the competence level of managers and staff, to identify root causes of problems, and to develop and implement action plans that enhance organizational/program/departmental effectiveness. Equal attention is paid to the technical issues and the human interactions involved in dealing with the technical issues. Consultants promote innovation, education, and continuous improvement throughout the organization.

Facilitating Teams

The quality consultant, through an understanding of group processes, assists in building collaborative relationships among employees throughout the organization. Through training and coaching interpersonal skills, communication, and conflict management, the quality consultant works toward creating an environment of trust among individuals and groups or teams. Teams exist within the organization in a variety of forms, including management teams, departmental teams, task forces, committees, and process improvement teams. Team effectiveness determines the speed and the quality of the results produced by the team. The quality consultant coaches team leaders and team members in problem-solving methods and tools, evaluates team strengths and weaknesses, provides feedback, and facilitates teams through the 3-phase quality management integration process.

Training

A quality consultant supports the development of a "learning organization" by promoting a wide variety of learning opportunities. Consultants provide staff development opportunities that meet identified organizational, team, and individual needs, incorporating principles of adult learning to design and deliver effective training. They produce training materials, resources, and job aids that support learning and design training modes that easily transfer to the job.

Consultants often coach others who are responsible for training (e.g., staff developers, managers, quality coordinators) in effective training strategies. They also assist managers in developing job orientation programs that ensure consistent, effective job training for new employees. Professional training for quality managers and QMI coordinators may include the training and quality manager certification that is described in the display on pages 121–122.

Process Planning and QMI

The quality consultant is responsible for the integration of a system for improving organizational processes. The system is designed to locate decision-making and problem-solving responsibilities as close to the information sources and relevant resources as possible.

Lifelong learning and professional development are strategic goals for human resources' development and staff retention. QMI coordinators and quality management leaders will find a thorough overview of quality concepts and tools in the certification training for quality managers offered by the American Society for Quality (ASQ). ASQ organizes the CQM body of knowledge as follows (the concepts are closely related to QMI concepts):

I. Quality Standards
   A. Total Quality Management
   B. Continuous Quality Improvement
   C. Cycle Time Reduction
   D. Supplier Management
   E. Customer Service
   F. Quality Awards/Quality Standards Criteria (e.g., Baldrige, ISO 9000)

II. Organizations and Their Functions
   A. Organizational Assessment
   B. Organizational Structures
   C. Quality Functions Within the Organization
   D. Communication Within the Organization
   E. Change Agents and Their Effects on Organizations
   F. Management Styles
   G. Business Functions

III. Quality Needs and Overall Strategic Plans
   A. Linkage Between Quality Function Needs and Overall Strategic Plan
   B. Linkage Between Strategic Plan and Quality Plan
   C. Theory of Variation (common and special causes)
   D. Quality Function Mission
   E. Priority of Quality Function Within the Organization
   F. Metrics and Goals that Drive Organizational Performance
   G. Formulation of Quality Principles and Policies
   H. Resource Requirements to Manage the Quality Function

IV. Customer Satisfaction and Focus
   A. Types of Customers (e.g., internal, external, end-user)
   B. Elements of Customer-Driven Organizations
   C. Customer Expectations, Priorities, Needs, and "Voice"
   D. Customer Relationship Management and Commitment (e.g., complaints, feedback, corrective action)
   E. Customer Identification and Segmentation
   F. Partnership and Alliances Between Customers and Suppliers
   G. Communication Techniques (e.g., surveys, focus groups)
   H. Multiple-Customer Management and Conflict Resolution
   I. Customer Retention/Loyalty

V. Project Management
   A. Planning
   B. Implementation

VI. Continuous Improvement
   A. Tools

        B.   Cost of Quality
        C.   Process Improvement
        D.   Trend Analysis
        E.   Measurement Issues
        F.   Concurrent Engineering and Process Mapping

VII. Human Resources Management
        A.   Leadership Roles and Responsibilities
        B.   Quality Staffing Issues
        C.   Quality Responsibilities in Job/Position Descriptions
        D.   Post-Training Evaluation and Reinforcement
        E.   Team Formation and Evolution
        F.   Team Management

VIII. Training and Education
        A.   Importance of Top-Down Support and Strategic Planning for Quality Training
        B.   Training Subgroups and Topics
        C.   Training Needs Analysis
        D.   Post-Training Evaluation and Reinforcement
        E.   Tools

This certification and others in the quality management fields are offered twice a year around the United States by ASQ. Previous examinees have come from many different quality-related jobs such as CQI coordinator, quality director, administrator, department manager, or CEO. To purchase training materials or for a free copy of the sample questions from CQM examinations and the CQM Body of Knowledge, contact ASQ ([800] 248-1946).

Working with management teams, process improvement teams, and department teams, the quality consultant aids in the development of monitoring tools and data collection methodology. Consultants coach teams and individuals in using the tools that support process improvement efforts, including flowcharts, cause–and–effect diagrams, run charts, and statistical process control. Consultants assist with the collection and review of measurement data on process outputs. Recognizing that many processes cross department lines, the consultant works toward enhanced collaboration between interdependent persons and groups within the organization.

Structure and Systems Design

The quality consultant assesses organizational structure and systems to determine their impact on the quality management philosophy and makes recommendations for changes that move the organization toward alignment with quality management procedures. A consultant uses and teaches systems thinking to enable management to monitor and deal proactively with internal and external influences on organizational effectiveness.

. . .

Base the decision to employ a quality consultant on the organization's culture, whether anyone is available internally, whether some permanent centralized oversight of the QMI process or of budget issues is desired, and other considerations. Whatever is done, consider the strategic plans, and then make the decision to proceed.

Assessing the Breadth and Depth
of QMI Deployment in an Organization

Strategic planning for the organization is a central and ongoing activity for both the quality council and the senior management team. As QMI principles begin to be implemented, the facility's quality council may choose to use the Assessment Tool for QMI Deployment (Appendix M). The assessment tool is based on many of the QMI implementation guidelines found in Chapter 1. Various factors are addressed for each of the six QMI core concepts, including one or more data-based factors for successful QMI implementation in each concept area. Later, periodic assessment of the QMI deployment provides ongoing measurement of the facility's progress. In addition, the relative success of various organizational segments such as departments or facilities can be compared.

Woodland Care Center: A Postscript

Any "real-life" narrative of QMI must include the possibility of an imperfect implementation. In fact, we can learn lessons on the need for leadership commitment (the first potential internal barrier in Chapter 4) from the Woodland Care Center case study:

> Approximately 6–8 weeks after the end of the initial QMI project at Woodland Care Center, we contacted Woodland's administrator. We wanted to know how things were going—had momentum been maintained in implementing the new concepts? The administrator's answer reinforced the importance of the first critical issue in the process of implementing a cultural change such as QMI, steady management attention to continuous process improvement, and the barrier that may arise when top managers' support is unclear.
>
> QMI implementation had slowed to a crawl, waiting for clear corporate direction from Woodland's parent organization. The topmost corporate management continued its pursuit of QMI organization-wide, for which it is to be commended. This multifacility, national organization hired a full-time champion, a former director of nursing in long-term care facilities with experience in QMI, to direct the QMI effort—a clear message of corporate commitment. Until that person was installed and familiar with organization processes and culture, however, Woodland Care Center slowed its implementation effort. All but one facility in the national group stalled on their journeys to QMI until corporate leadership became active again.
>
> As a result of this time lag, some department heads lost interest and momentum in their own quality efforts. In particular, Woodland's quality council lost its oversight role as it waited for the desired structure for the new organization's quality efforts to be made clear. Additional effort is required from the administrator, who must maintain progress alone, without the collaborative support she anticipated from the organization's management team after its initial QMI training the previous year.
>
> To the credit of the administrator, department heads continued their second round of department quality improvement projects, and there have been successes in the third-floor short-term care unit. She continues to raise issues regarding customer service and resident focus. This is an excellent way to reinforce the potential gains of process change, through the use of QMI tools and techniques. Many department heads also are using a reference library on quality tools and implementation that was developed in-house to move ahead and solve the identified department problems. For example, several are

developing process flowcharts of their key department processes. Others are waiting for a corporate policy, however, and some projects such as collecting demographic statistics are on hold because of a change in personnel.

Efforts in installing quality improvement processes often go on without being formally labeled "QMI." In fact, you will discover that TQM or CQI (by any name) is simply the most practical and responsive way to manage process costs effectively and consistently, to meet residents' long-term clinical needs, and to satisfy internal customers. These are the ultimate goals of QMI, employee involvement, and management by fact processes. With QMI, care providers can give the quality of care that their customers expect: cost-effective and efficient.

Woodland's early long-term focus seemed to be a general acknowledgment that processes can and should be more effective and flow more smoothly. As in most health care settings, at Woodland there already was an expectation of continuous improvement of patient outcomes. The next phase of quality council and department head attention should be methodical process measurement and goal setting. Many well-intentioned QMI efforts have bogged down after initial strategic planning, and QMI communications efforts lose their early momentum.

The prognosis for Woodland's QMI journey is very optimistic. The staff, with strong support from their administrator, continue to explore QMI concepts with energy, healthy skepticism, and intelligent consideration at the department and cross-functional levels. The months and years ahead promise exciting and challenging changes for the staff and residents as the staff continue their quality journey, albeit temporarily at the department level. The residents and Woodland's other customer groups should experience improved customer satisfaction and a slower growth of health care costs.

Five Great Reasons to Implement QMI

Although there are critical issues to address and barriers to overcome when initiating QMI processes, the alternative of not implementing QMI presents long-term care providers with some serious considerations:

1. As consumer knowledge and expectations increase, the demand for consistent high-quality care and service also increase. Failure to deliver what customers demand is costly and is usually evidenced through a declining census and a poor reputation within the community. QMI ensures that customer needs are monitored frequently and receive a prompt response.

2. The acceleration of change requires that organizations be flexible. The inflexibility of traditional bureaucracy results in organizational rigidity and a sluggish response to change. Because QMI involves both management and staff in continual process evaluation and improvement, organizations recognize quality shifts sooner and respond to problems with broad staff support. Organizations become more nimble during transitions.

3. A departmental approach to managing a facility reduces the facility's ability to deliver customer-focused high-quality care and service. Using a departmental approach, department managers strive to optimize their own department, often at another department's expense. Until departmental barriers are reduced, the focus remains on "what's best for my department" rather than "what's best for the customer." QMI's systems orientation bypasses the limitations caused by departmental shortsightedness.

4. Economic pressures to operate long-term care facilities more efficiently are felt increasingly as managed care takes center stage. Without a system such as QMI to continuously find and implement better methods, the facility will find that competitors are capturing the managed care market.

5. The belief that the facility's management team is the best group to solve all of the problems and make all of the decisions ultimately prevents sustainable, long-term solutions. This small group of people cannot possibly possess all of the information needed for permanent solutions. Problems may go away for a little while, but the same problems will come back to haunt the organization unless managers obtain input and involvement from those who know the details of the issues—usually the direct care and service providers and the customers themselves. QMI actively involves both customers and care providers in decision making for long-term process improvements.

Status of QMI Implementations: Questions Remain

Additional development and implementation studies are needed on the status of QMI implementation in long-term care. These sorts of studies are necessary if organizations want to manage risk and to satisfy customer needs in managed care environments. Examples of QMI topics include the following.

Process Measurement Issues

- Establishing which metrics and health care process improvements are most highly correlated with QMI success
- Measuring the success of QMI implementation by studying changes that resulted from training (e.g., at intervals of 6, 9, and 12 months)
- Creating systems that track process outcomes, then setting thresholds that trigger corrective action for process problems
- Selecting metrics that provide the best process management in a QMI environment and best analysis of customer needs

Organizational Development and Human Relations

- Identifying the most effective means to address anxiety among supervisors, middle managers, and employees in organizations undergoing affiliations or other network activities
- Determining issues that cause rapid job turnover among the least-educated employees, such as nursing assistants and dietary aides, and finding a win-win situation for this group's involvement in QMI implementation
- Planning and scheduling time for training and team activities
- Deciding whether the organization requires/desires full-time QMI staff (studies differ in their recommendations about how senior they should be to provide authority for implementation)
- Designing organization and employee strategies to support effective, cost-efficient QMI implementation
- Studying staff retention, management turnover, and other variables that reflect organizational impact of QMI implementation

Customer Issues

- Confirming that interpersonal relationships are the greatest determinants of resident and family satisfaction, and identifying the specific component factors that are the best predictors of total customer satisfaction
- Studying the most effective means of balancing needs of residents and families/friends against those of regulatory agencies and payer groups
- Studying clinical benefits for residents that result from improved process tracking
- Identifying how application, admissions, and discharge patterns have shifted in the health care marketplace and in competing long-term care facilities
- Identifying key requirements of all customer groups and clarifying their differences (e.g., long-term versus short-term residents)

Summary

This book has provided guidelines for the QMI journey, introducing QMI principles and processes as they apply to long-term care. The importance of sturdy support for QMI on the part of senior staff at individual facilities was emphasized, with a discussion of corporate or national leadership support as well. Management's role as coach and champion promotes continuous quality improvement through QMI so that regulatory requirements are identified as minimal standards of acceptable care, not merely as desirable targets. The "new" health care environment requires flexibility, process consistency among direct care providers and other employee groups, and effective strategic quality planning. QMI provides "profound knowledge" (Deming's term) of processes.

Using QMI manages risk and provides robust long-term care processes in an environment that includes rapid change, affiliations between organizations, stressful working conditions for employees at all levels of health care organizations, and changed expectations and standards in health care for residents. The purpose of strategic planning should be customer satisfaction, particularly to gain optimal, long-term clinical outcomes for residents.

The measurable results that can be anticipated following the implementation of QMI include reductions in costs of quality; improved competitive position in the long-term care industry, due to increased customer satisfaction; improved job satisfaction and quality of work life for employees and management; and reduced employee turnover. Most significant among measurable results, however, are the anticipated improvements in residents' long-term health care. Care providers (employees), regulatory agencies, and payer groups all benefit from this improvement.

Such improvements are particularly desirable because lengths of stay in facilities are growing shorter. Measurable indicators track variables such as clinical outcomes, employee satisfaction, and benchmark data from competitors or from sister facilities within a single national group. Using such QMI data provides systematic strategic planning, process improvement, and data-driven policies and procedures.

It is hoped that the status quo expectations in government regulatory and reimbursement systems will shift to methods that encourage constant improvements in resident outcomes and reward improved cost effectiveness when implemented appropriately. Government policies need to change with accelerating flexibility and rapidity because resident/family expectations are changing rapidly. Some experts believe that families have always expected rehabilitation and maximal independence for their loved ones but that the system of medical professionals, government regulators, and payer groups inadvertently prevented these outcomes. These are the goals of all QMI implementations such as Woodland's, and they benefit any staff members or customers who are involved in health care systems in the future, however those systems may develop.

APPENDIXES

Appendix A
The 3-Phase Quality Management Integration Process

Phase 1—Priorities, Strategies, and Objectives
- Identify desired outcomes and goals for the QMI process
- Conduct preliminary needs assessment in departments and at local sites
  - Management roles
  - Employees' and supervisors' perceptions of quality
  - Current data: history of regulatory compliance, customer or employee satisfaction surveys, clinical data, and so forth
- Prioritize or modify goals

Phase 2—Implementing the Quality Improvement Process
- Communicate purposes of quality management process to organization
- Establish quality structure: quality council, management roles
- Conduct training in basic quality principles
  - Managers/supervisors, followed by employee groups
- Identify key management/supervisory processes and measurements
- Identify customer needs
- Determine critical success factors and establish a system to measure them
- Initiate projects selected by quality council

Phase 3—Continuous Improvement of the Quality Management Process
- Maintain momentum!
- Expand scope of participation throughout organization
- Establish clear accountability in management and employee groups for implementing QMI concepts in daily work life
- Monitor process and outcome measures to drive planning and decision making
- Ensure effective communication systems throughout the organization
- Refine and reassess success of QMI process continually
- Reexamine customer needs, concerns, and results at frequent, scheduled intervals

© 1996 Maryjane G. Bradley and Nancy R. Thompson.

Appendix B
Executives' and Managers' Guide to Integration of New Quality Management Culture

Senior Executives' Nondelegable Roles[1]

The new impetus for quality will be limited only by the pace at which our CEOs accept responsibility for their nondelegable roles. There are seven steps that a responsible CEO must take to achieve quality in any organization. They are strikingly similar to the steps that CEOs already routinely take in managing for financial results:

1. Set up and serve on the company's quality council, the quality equivalent of the finance committee.
2. Establish corporate quality goals, including quality improvement goals, and make them a part of the business plan.
3. Make provisions for training the entire company hierarchy in managing for quality.
4. Establish the means to measure quality results against quality goals.
5. Review quality results against goals on a regular basis.
6. Give recognition for superior quality performance.
7. Revise the reward system to respond to the changes demanded by world-class quality.

Managing for Quality[2]

- The entire management hierarchy must be trained in how to manage for quality.
- Upper managers must personally take charge of managing for quality, much as they have long done in managing for finance. (This puts a limit on what they may delegate.)
- The business plan must be enlarged to include quality goals.
- Managing for quality must be integrated into managing the business.
- Quality improvement must become an ongoing process, year after year.
- New measures must be developed to enable upper managers to follow the progress of parameters such as customer satisfaction, competitive quality, performance of business processes, cost of poor quality, and so forth.
- The work force must be given the training and empowerment needed to enable them to participate widely in job planning and improvement.
- The reward system must be revised to take account of the changes in job functions and responsibility.

References

1   Juran, J.M. (1993, July–August). Made in USA—A renaissance in quality. *Harvard Business Review.*

2   Juran, J.M. (1994, August). The upcoming century of quality. *Quality Progress,* 29–37.

Appendix C
Health Care Criteria for Performance Excellence—1999
A Framework for Organization Self-Assessment[1]

Health care organizations may use the Malcolm Baldrige National Quality Award framework either to guide their implementation of quality management integration (QMI) or to apply for the annual award. The 1999 vocabulary and concepts relate to QMI in health care, in both for-profit and not-for-profit organizations. (Like the Education Criteria, these are industry-specific versions of the seven "Business" Baldrige Criteria in vocabulary and concepts.) Improvement activities in all seven criteria should address communications, root cause analysis, corrective action, process measurement and improvement, and cost-of-quality analysis.

1. Leadership
    1.1 Leadership System
    1.2 Public Responsibility and Citizenship
2. Strategic Planning
    2.1 Strategy Development Process
    2.2 Organizational Strategy
3. Focus on Patients, Other Customers, and Markets
    3.1 Patient/Customer and Health Care Market Knowledge
    3.2 Patient/Customer Satisfaction and Relationship Enhancement
4. Information and Analysis
    4.1 Selection and Use of Information and Data
    4.2 Selection and Use of Comparative Information and Data
    4.3 Analysis and Review of Organizational Performance
5. Staff Focus
    5.1 Work Systems
    5.2 Staff Education, Training, and Development
    5.3 Staff Well-Being and Satisfaction
6. Process Management
    6.1 Design and Delivery of Health Care
    6.2 Management of Support Processes
7. Organizational Performance Results
    7.1 Patient/Customer Satisfaction Results
    7.2 Health Care Results
    7.3 Financial and Market Results
    7.4 Staff and Work Systems Results
    7.5 Organization-Specific Results

Activities for QMI[2]

Activities	Examples
1. Leadership	Management vision and leadership
	Quality council guidance
	Coordination of project teams and projects
	Resource allocation
2. Strategic Planning	Planning continuous improvement for the short and long term
	Deploying plans to all areas of organization
3. Focus on Patients, Other Customers, and Markets	Establish systems that provide knowledge of customer and competitive marketplace
	Measures of customer satisfaction and methods of dealing with customer dissatisfaction
4. Information and Analysis	Managing and using data to drive continuous quality improvement of systems and processes throughout organization
5. Staff Focus	Involving and enabling entire workforce
	Recognizing and celebrating personal and organizational successes
	Ensuring communications: quality awareness, education/training, flow of quality information throughout organization
6. Process Management	Systems and processes are designed to deliver continuous quality improvement
	Internal processes such as business and support services, supplier quality, and quality assessment are addressed
7. Organizational Performance Results	Products and services are assessed and results of performance are measured
	Data analyze levels and trends in key product/service outcomes

References

1   Baldrige National Quality Program. (1999). *Health care criteria for performance excellence*.
2   These activities illustrate the seven categories of the Malcolm Baldrige National Quality Award, Criteria for Performance Excellence, 1999. Appendix J contains more information.

Appendix D
Data-Driven QMI: A Mini-Handbook

This appendix contains several sets of indicators and other implementation ideas for using data-driven decision making in your facility and supplements information provided throughout this book, in particular, Chapter 6. Remember that data are at the heart of the six core concepts in the QMI model, as well as the Plan–Do–Study–Act (PDSA) cycle, the 3-phase quality management integration process, and most QMI tools and techniques.

Suggested CQI Areas[1]

If you are wrestling with starting the QMI data management process, here are some ways to gather information, set standards (targets), and track outcomes.

Quality of care

Pressure sores
Contractures
Infection rates
Assessments
   Risk (fall, skin, nutrition)
   Initial
Change of condition
   Response time
   Notification
   Nursing judgment
Plans of care
   Timely, measurable goals
   Interdisciplinary approaches
   Resident centered

Drive care delivery
Restraints
   Chemical
   Physical
Weight loss
Medication administration
Documentation
   Accurate picture of resident
   Responses to treatments/plan of care
   Identification of changes (acute and significant)
   Restorative measures and response
   Timely notes reflecting good nursing judgment

Quality of life

Food/dining experience
   Temperature
   Correct/accurate diets
   Quality
Resident council responses
Psychosocial response
Activities

Environmental
   Laundry
   Housekeeping
   Clean/safe
Resident rights
   Staff interaction
   Resident choice

Data Collection—A 1-Minute Lesson[2]

Although data collection is important, it is not always necessary. In addition, you may not need to collect new data because the data that you need may already exist.

Collect New Data

1. If the solution to the problem is not clear
2. If you have taken action three times and the problem still exists
3. If the wrong solution will make things worse

Use Existing Data

1. If the data relate to the characteristics or problems with which you are concerned
2. If the data use the same measures you are concerned with
3. If the processes that created the data have not changed since they were collected (equipment, personnel, and processes are the same)
4. If new data can still be collected in the same way as the existing data

Data Collection Pointers for QMI

Uses of Data in QMI Projects

Data may be used to display levels and trends. Pictured on a graph, as so many quality data are, levels are individual data points that have been counted or measured. When those points are connected over time, trends or other nonrandom patterns may appear. These outcomes of data analysis teach the QMI practitioner about the process being measured. Follow-up activities are then based on what Scholtes and associates' *The Team Handbook* calls management by fact.[3] The information gained from this exercise allows employees or managers to understand their process more deeply and thereby identify what is actually happening in their process, not what originally was planned to happen. This is the beginning of examination of the common causes that are active in the system rather than the special causes that are unique situations, as described in Chapter 2.

A letter from W. Edwards Deming[4] in *The Team Handbook* includes information on process variation:

> *A stable process, one with no indication of a special cause of variation, is said to be . . . in statistical control or stable with respect to the quality characteristic measured. It is a random process. Its behavior in the near future is predictable. Of course some unforeseen jolt may come along and knock the process out of statistical control. A system that is in statistical control has a definable identity and a definable capability. . . . Improvement of a stable process requires fundamental change in the system. . . . We should try to reduce variation of a stable system [i.e., "process improvement" on the common cause system].*

If one particular special cause requires frequent fire fighting, it is no longer "special"; it is part of the everyday common cause system. Beyond the prevention of special cause problems, care providers should address shifting the entire common cause process to a new level by continuous process improvement. The common cause system can be identified only by measuring present outcomes and looking for trends. To this end, Stofac encouraged health care providers to track, trend, and categorize data.

To *categorize* is to consider subgroups when collecting data. *Stratification* and *segmentation* also describe this process of considering subgroups against one another or versus the total population. For example, Bednar and Reeves (see Chapter 4) differentiated between barriers perceived by upper and lower management levels. Survey data at Abbey View show some differences between floors but only on certain questions. Graphs of results may look very different when teams compare results for the total organization against subtotals from individual departments. Differences exist among groups of employees, groups of customers, or paperwork processes. QMI practitioners should be sensitive to differing results among groups that may be masked when totals are aggregated or to differences between similar processes that help to focus process improvement efforts. See the section "Segmentation and Aggregation of Data" in Chapter 6 for further discussion of segmentation, an important QMI technique.

All decisions about process improvement should be made by considering the ultimate benefits to customers. All such decisions affect customers, even when the purpose is to benefit internal customers. As discussed in Chapter 4, health care providers may resist measuring their own work processes, but measuring patient outcomes is both acceptable and familiar in the health care industry. Thus, data collection and analysis in your organization may start more comfortably by measuring the clinical outcomes of various subgroups of residents.

Using Survey Data

Survey data are opinion data. As such, they are more subjective, more difficult to predict, and sometimes more difficult to respond to than objective measurements of tangible product characteristics. With the major role played by service processes, we must ask customers about their needs and then respond to what they tell us. To be successful, therefore, we must be thoughtful in selecting questions that will represent their true feelings and will define customer priorities so that we can ensure that our processes provide both satisfactory outcomes and cost-effective, productive systems of production. These factors of success apply to both manufacturing and service processes.

When you change a service process in response to survey results, you are changing the common cause system that determines those results. That is why survey data help to drive improvements in process delivery and customer satisfaction for long-term care customer groups.

Appendixes E and F provide four sets of surveys. Although they have not been validated scientifically, the surveys provide samples of the types of information that may be measured. For very large organizations or multifacility organizations, more sophisticated questionnaire development and scoring should be employed; complex results may be compared and stored in extensive databases. Appendix E includes the questionnaire that was used both before and after the introduction of QMI principles and tools to Woodland Care Center's leadership team. The QMI survey results from Woodland senior staff (see also Chapters 3 and 6) indicated a strong overall improvement of 19% in their response to attitudes about implementing QMI, with individual responses improving from 11% to 27%.

As data are collected, it is important to compare them appropriately. For example, using the identical survey for pre- and postevaluation provided continuity at Woodland. Data from both evaluations were compared and a baseline established against which the results of later surveys could be compared. Authors of the survey should remain alert for potential bias in survey questions and data analysis. Unlike the senior staff's evaluations at Woodland, Abbey View's survey (Appendix F) was addressed to one particular group of customers, the family members/designated caregivers/concerned friends of residents. Surveys are often an effective means of tapping this group's reactions to and suggestions for improvement of a facility's services. A consulting team developed and administered this survey. They then completed many statistical analyses of the results. (To learn more of the statistical details, see the feature "For the Data Lovers Among Us" in Appendix F. Details on survey techniques are illustrated in Appendixes E and F and in Chapter 6, as is the usefulness of electronic databases and computer analysis.)

All survey results should be reported to respondents. It is unethical to report only the favorable responses; negative information focuses attention on the opportunity to improve processes, and employees and customers understand that. At a later time, how processes changed in response to what was learned can be reported.

QMI includes the data collection and data analysis tools that allow organizations to study process variation and measure the effectiveness of their QMI initiatives. Data analysis permits periodic monitoring of process changes and the directing of resources to process improvements that are determined to be of the highest priority. Setting standards for performance enables departments and teams to set thresholds that trigger corrective action. Eventually, effective data collection allows organizations to understand their processes, so that they can manage risk and control process costs per resident. They may study demographics, clinical outcomes, care delivery processes, psychosocial trends, and financial performance. Examples of the variables that may be measured are listed in this appendix and in Chapter 6. Management should begin cautiously with a limited number of key indicators and should focus on data collection in the key processes.

Ensuring Compliance with Regulators by Studying Process and Outcome Data

The survey process of annual, unscheduled compliance surveys by the state is an inspection, or quality control, process. In the past, compliance surveys typically measured whether specific quality assurance processes had been drafted rather than measured their deployment or their outcomes. The survey process that is current as of this writing uses quality indicator information taken from the Minimum Data Set to focus on potential problem areas within the facility. The purpose of the survey process is to ensure continued maintenance of standards ("zero defects"), but it does not emphasize the continuous process improvement that keeps organizations effective, efficient, and competitive. The survey process reflects an assurance or quality control approach rather than continuous quality improvement (CQI), and it inhibits improvements of processes and outcomes.

Results Justify Investment in QMI Data Collection

Customer and employee satisfaction, optimal clinical outcomes for residents, and improved organizational performance and competitiveness are goals for QMI data collection and process improvement efforts. These successes justify the expenditures of time and resources on QMI efforts.

Outcomes Management in Health Care: The Search for What Works[5]

There are research-based links among symptoms, diagnoses, treatments, and outcomes. Clinical protocols can be developed that link types and length of treatment to diagnoses. Links are less clear in processes that address behavior change activities or processes that interact. Nevertheless, we seek these cause-and-effect links between processes and outcomes.

Selected outcomes and assessments should include the following:

- Segmentation (stratification) of the population to allow analysis of which interventions work best
- Specified action steps (processes) that lead to documented improved outcomes (change model)
- Select measures that reflect results in the short, medium, and long term, for which the organization is truly accountable
- Standards, practice guidelines, and treatment/service interventions that are valid indicators, in addition to customer needs and satisfaction factors
- Service effectiveness indicators may measure at least four "families" of outcomes: increase in functioning (physical health, emotional health, cognitive functioning), maintenance of functioning and emotional health, prevention of additional problems or relapses, and slowing of a progressively deteriorating condition
- Risk-adjusted outcomes in demographic or other population segments are examined, taking into consideration differences between segments
- Outcomes that are linked with cost when determining effectiveness and efficiency
- Practical, focused training and supervisory procedures that are centered around selected outcomes
- Application of measures and assessments that are appropriate to the specific population segment (e.g., age, gender, current health conditions)
- Selection of outcomes that support prevention and early intervention as cost-effective strategies are favored

Managed care models use strategies and approaches that may benefit long-term care. These will enhance both resident outcomes and administrative results; for example:

- Aggressive gatekeeping (to better predict appropriate admissions decisions)
- Utilization management (to use facility resources and staff effectively)
- Integrated case management (to optimize resident outcomes through collaboration among facility staff)
- Negotiated case and or capitation structures for payment (to use in discussions with payer and regulatory groups)
- Promotion and documentation of successful procedures and activities (to enable other staff to duplicate effective processes)

Processes Data versus Outcomes Data in Health Care

Organizations are asked more and more often to demonstrate outcome improvements rather than whether processes or policies exist. In other words, can the organization actually deploy the plans that were drafted and then measure the results? Can the data prove the facility's successful care of individuals and organization management?

Example of a formerly acceptable (i.e., pre-QMI) procedure statement: "A system is in place to address emergencies in our building and maintenance."

The indicator to document this statement might be that policies exist regarding the people who and organizations that monitor the building's 24-hour on-call response system. But are the policies followed? Does proof—data—exist? This approach to process management is a quality control/quality assurance approach. Alternatively, QMI focuses on determining whether the policy is a priority for the maintenance staff or is in the cross-functional emergency system. If it is a priority, then an indicator would be tracked and the system made as fail-safe as possible. This process is referred to as the "prevention" of problems such as unnecessary setup time, rework, or waste of materials. An important aspect of QMI is that the process or system is regularly monitored for potential problems and for improvements.

Example of QMI approach: "A checksheet documents certain aspects of the building's 24-hour on-call response system at an established interval."

The checksheet would document data collection for appropriate individuals to know whether the procedures that are established are followed and whether they should be improved. Other QMI tools also could apply. Efforts should be focused on a few core systems and processes and on key indicators.

The questions that supplement the initial question "Does a process or policy exist?" are those that point to why a QMI approach should be employed: Can the indicators that are followed regularly direct one to quantitative outcomes that prove excellence of care for individuals and demonstrate effective management processes? Are priorities established based on data to serve key customer segments or core processes? Are QMI guidelines established in a nonblaming, nonpunishing environment?

Effective Use of Data

- Seek usefulness, not perfection
- Act now; do not wait for computer support
- Use sampling
- Use both quantitative and qualitative data; quantitative data are preferred
- Develop a balanced set of measures
- Use outcomes/results, mid-process outcomes, and ongoing process measures
- Plot data through time; look for trends and shifts that indicate a change in the process' common cause system
- Stratify (subgroup) data to obtain a clearer picture and to target improvements
- Use data that already have been collected whenever possible
- Select indicators that measure variation in core processes and in areas that have been designated as organizational priorities
- Measure key customer satisfaction and dissatisfaction indicators, then respond to them
- Measure critical risk factors
- Measure supplier performance (performance has an impact on the entire system's outcomes) and communicate results to the suppliers
- Identify process bottlenecks—otherwise, other process improvements simply cause backlogs at the bottlenecks; eliminating bottlenecks reflects a systems orientation

References

1   Stofac, T.J. (1994). *Continuous quality initiatives: A manager's guide* (p. 73). Des Moines, IA: Briggs Corporation.
2   Joiner Associates, Inc. (1994, Fall). One-minute lesson: Data collection. *Managing for Quality.*
3   Scholtes, P.R. et al. (Eds.). (1988). *The team handbook* (pp. 2–15). Madison, WI: Joiner Associates. The book contains straightforward, user-friendly guidelines for teams and managers on data collection implementation.

4   Deming, W.E. (1988). In P.R. Scholtes et al. (Eds.), *The team handbook* (p. 15). Madison, WI: Joiner Associates.

5   Pecora. P.J. et al. (1997, April). Measuring outcomes in the changing environment of child welfare services. *Child and Family Focus.*

Appendix E
QMI Survey Results: Woodland Care Center
Pre- and Postevaluations

It is always worthwhile to study the data that have been collected both before a process change, to establish the necessity for improvement, and after the change is implemented, to assess success periodically. This approach was chosen for Woodland Care Center's introductory QMI project. (There is further discussion of the use of survey data in Appendix D and Chapter 6, and Woodland's survey also is discussed in Chapters 3 and 4.)

The results from Woodland's survey reflect the senior staff's assessment of barriers, issues, and attitudes that will affect implementation of QMI in the facility. The survey questions were developed for use during initial QMI training as pre- and postevaluations of the project. Pre-evaluation survey results were obtained from 15 senior staff members during two 1-day QMI training sessions. Post-evaluations were collected 10 weeks later at a department head meeting that was conducted at the conclusion of the initial QMI implementation activities.

The first set of responses rated overall satisfaction on a 10-point scale. The following six questions were open-ended, assessing barriers, issues, and attitudes. Responses were grouped in clusters and counted; these were sorted by number of responses (Pareto analysis). Responses with the highest degree of consensus were reported as issues to be considered by the administrator, the department heads, and the quality council.

Interpretation of Results

Because postevaluation results were based on nine individuals' responses, it was recommended that the quality council conduct a second survey in 6 months to ensure hearing from the entire group. These data also would document whether the indicated culture changes were long-lasting rather than short range. A strong 19% improvement in positive ratings on the five questions was determined overall. The small number of responses may have caused some positive bias through self-selection of the respondents. Based on conversations with several senior staff members and the administrator, however, the 19% gain seemed appropriate.

Quality Management Integration (QMI)
Survey—Woodland Care Center

1.   Define "quality" at Woodland Care Center.

2.   How do you feel we rate for overall quality now that QMI has been implemented? (Ratings: 10 High–1 Low)
    Management support for quality: _____
    Staff support for quality: _____

We measure and study our work process performance: _____
Departments support one another for quality of resident care: _____

Barriers and Actions
1. List three barriers to acceptance of QMI in your work area.

2. List two actions that demonstrate senior management support for QMI that are visible to employees.

3. List two actions that senior staff can take to support or collaborate with other departments.

4. What is one action you can take tomorrow/Monday to help encourage your department to implement QMI?

QMI survey results

| | (Ratings: 10 = High, 1 = Low) | | | |
Quality management now	Project start, average	Standard deviation	Project after 10 weeks, average	Standard deviation
How does the facility rate in terms of overall quality now?	5.32	.91	6.78	1.39
How would you rate management's support of QMI?	7.12	1.5	8.0	2.1
How would you rate staff's support of QMI?	4.54	1.32	6.22	1.48
How would you rate the facility's ability to measure and study work process performance?	4.86	1.63	5.78	1.48
How would you rate interdepartmental support of quality of resident care?	5.0	2.0	6.33	1.22
Overall average	5.37	1.47	6.62	1.53

Barriers and Actions
The following nine responses come from the 10-week postevaluations.

1. List three barriers to acceptance of QMI in your work area.
    Time   6 (67%)
    Reluctance to change   4 (44%)
    Comments: "Time management skills." "People need to develop solutions, not just identify problems." "Holds employees accountable . . . (managers too!)."
2. List two actions that employees look for that demonstrate senior management's support of QMI.
    Involvement/cooperate with employees   7 (78%)
    Comments: "Use authority to make a decision; then follow up to be sure it is done." "Role model." "They look for results."

3. List two actions that senior staff can take to support or collaborate with other departments.

Support one another	6 (67%)
Communicate	4 (44%)
Be open-minded	3 (33%)

    Comments: "When conflict arises with other departments, be open and proactive." "Show appreciation of new ideas." "Look at our own department's responsibility."
4. What is one action that you can take tomorrow or Monday to help start your department on its quality journey?

Start another project	3 (33%)
Continue frequent/weekly meetings	3 (33%)

    Comments: "Keep QMI on the front burner." "Ask staff to problem-solve with me; come to solutions together that work out for the floor." "Display consistent positive attitude toward QMI."

Define "Quality" at Woodland Care Center

Exceeding resident, family, and corporate expectations for services provided at Woodland

Improving continuously in all areas of customer service, both in response to existing problems and proactively anticipating customers' and staff needs

Doing the best you know how

Meeting customers' expectations

All customer groups sharing common goals of enhancing residents' lives, meeting their needs in a caring and supportive environment; we should be open and proactive

Giving the best possible care that residents can receive

Providing excellent resident care, with employees who care about one another

Trying for perfection

Providing high-quality care, at the same time promoting customer service at all levels

Recommendations from Consultant to Quality Council and Administrator (project after 10 weeks)

Study these responses and focus follow-on activities and discussions to deal with staff priority issues.

Maintain momentum with QMI projects and communications efforts. Note the 19% (strong) average improvement in results since the preevaluation in Week 1. Results from each question:

Quality management now	Gains over project life
How does the facility rate in terms of overall quality now?	+22%
How would you rate management's support of QMI?	+11%
How would you rate staff's support of QMI?	+27%
How would you rate the facility's ability to measure and study work process performance?	+16%
How would you rate interdepartmental support of quality of resident care?	+21%
Overall averages	+19%

Recommendations from Consultant to Woodland's Administrator and Managers

Priority Issue 1: Help staff and employees wrestle with allotting time for QMI. The response "too many projects at the same time" demonstrates a basic misunderstanding—QMI means systematic process improvement, which should be a part of all projects, even if they carry a different title. This is management by fact.

Because only 9 of 15 senior staff members completed the postevaluation survey, responses may have been biased. It is worth administering the survey again in 6 months during a meeting to ensure hearing options from the entire group. Note increased consensus in range of standard deviations; this may reflect bias in the smaller group. The results seem valid, however, based on comments made in surveys and discussions.

"Keep QMI on the front burner" (one response) could be the quality council's slogan!

Encourage staff to use data/statistics in similar, uncomplicated analyses of situations at Woodland.

Over a period of months "Communications" has dropped from Priority Issue 1 to Priority Issue 4. Congratulations on making a major breakthrough! This success is related to the strong improvement seen in interdepartmental support, reflecting responses in Question 3 and in other communications-related areas.

Appendix F
Family Satisfaction Surveys

It is important to survey family members, a separate customer group that has unique needs, regarding the quality of the customer service they received, in addition to surveying them to solicit their opinions on the quality of the treatment that their loved one received. The three surveys included here (Lakeland Family Survey, Opinion Survey,[1] and Family Satisfaction Opinion Survey: Abbey View Nursing Facility) have not been tested statistically for reliability (when consistent answers occur repeatedly) or for validity (when answers precisely represent the opinions of the survey's respondents), but they have been used in long-term care settings to gather data on levels of customer satisfaction among family members. The family satisfaction survey from Abbey View is complex and demonstrates a sophisticated statistical treatment of survey results by a consulting team. Further discussion of surveys and survey results, as well as Abbey View's results, are found in Chapter 6 and Appendixes D and E. Several resources are listed in Appendix J.

Lakeland Family Survey

This questionnaire was used for several years in an average-size facility that was part of a chain of facilities. Results were compared for changes or improvements from year to year. Later, chain administrators developed a common format for their family survey and then used the results to compare and improve processes at all of their facilities.

We are committed to providing high-quality care to the individuals we serve. We would like your feedback so that we may reinforce our strengths and eliminate or minimize our weaknesses. Your insights will be shared with the appropriate individuals. Your identity will remain confidential.

Directions: Answer each question using the 5-point scale below. Space is provided at the end of the questionnaire for your comments.

	Not applicable	Poor	Fair	Good	Excellent
1. How would you rate your initial contact?	1	2	3	4	5
2. Were you made aware of the services available at the facility?	1	2	3	4	5
3. Did staff refer you to the appropriate person when they were unable to answer your question(s)?	1	2	3	4	5
4. Did staff approach you with warmth and professionalism?	1	2	3	4	5
5. If you voiced a complaint, were you satisfied with the solution?	1	2	3	4	5

		Strongly Agree	Agree	Neutral	Disagree	Strongly disagree

6. Was the information that you received regarding your admission complete and understandable? 1 2 3 4 5

7. Did Social Services meet your needs during your residency and at the time you were discharged from the facility? 1 2 3 4 5

8. Did you receive good-quality nursing care? 1 2 3 4 5

9. Were the activities offered interesting to you? 1 2 3 4 5

10. Was your room clean? 1 2 3 4 5

11. Was the facility clean? 1 2 3 4 5

12. Were you satisfied with your rehabilitation program, including the resident education and treatment programs? 1 2 3 4 5

13. If you used the beauty shop, were the services offered satisfactory? 1 2 3 4 5

14. Were your meals served attractively, appealingly, and in a timely manner? 1 2 3 4 5

15. Was the facility and your room's temperature comfortable? 1 2 3 4 5

16. Were your experiences with volunteers pleasant and helpful? 1 2 3 4 5

17. Would you recommend the facility to others? 1 2 3 4 5

Comments:

Thank you for taking time to help us improve our service!

(Optional) If you would like us to contact you, please print your name and daytime telephone number in the space provided:

_____

_____

Customer Opinion Survey[1]

We are interested in your opinions about the services that we provide to residents. Please answer the following statements in a way that best sums up your opinion. For example, if you agree strongly with a given statement, then circle the number 1; if you have no particular opinion about a statement, then circle the number 3.

		Strongly Agree	Agree	Neutral	Disagree	Strongly disagree

In my opinion . . .

1. The assistants and aides like their jobs. 1 2 3 4 5

2. Most of the residents have adjusted to living in the nursing facility. 1 2 3 4 5

3.	The nursing staff understand how the residents feel.	1	2	3	4	5
4.	The nurses are well trained.	1	2	3	4	5
5.	The assistants and aides know what they are doing when providing care to residents.	1	2	3	4	5
6.	The staff care about the residents.	1	2	3	4	5
7.	The residents appear to be comfortable.	1	2	3	4	5
8.	The staff communicate well with everyone.	1	2	3	4	5
9.	Staff members are patient.	1	2	3	4	5
10.	The staff deal honestly with residents.	1	2	3	4	5
11.	A variety of meals are prepared.	1	2	3	4	5
12.	The dietitian is easy to talk with.	1	2	3	4	5
13.	The staff need to be more safety conscious.	1	2	3	4	5
14.	The food served to residents tastes good.	1	2	3	4	5
15.	The food servers are pleasant.	1	2	3	4	5
16.	The nursing facility is clean.	1	2	3	4	5
17.	The housekeeping department does a good job.	1	2	3	4	5
18.	The nursing facility has a bad odor.	1	2	3	4	5
19.	Housekeeping staff are pleasant to visit with.	1	2	3	4	5
20.	Activities that encourage thinking are made available to residents.	1	2	3	4	5
21.	The residents' property is often stolen and never recovered.	1	2	3	4	5
22.	The facility environment is uncomfortable.	1	2	3	4	5
23.	The chapel services are inadequate.	1	2	3	4	5
24.	The administration spends money wisely.	1	2	3	4	5
25.	If requested, residents can change roommates.	1	2	3	4	5
26.	If requested, residents can change their care.	1	2	3	4	5

I am satisfied with . . .

27.	The assistants' and aides' service	1	2	3	4	5
28.	The dietary service	1	2	3	4	5
29.	The nursing service	1	2	3	4	5
30.	The housekeeping service	1	2	3	4	5
31.	The facility's administration	1	2	3	4	5

For Residents Only

Please provide information about yourself. You may ask staff for assistance.

1. Sex   ____Male   ____Female
2. How long have you been a resident of this nursing facility?   ____ 0–6 months   ____ 7–11 months   ____ 1–3 years   ____ 4–6 years   ____ More than 6 years
3. Is this the first time that you have been a resident of a nursing facility?
   ____Yes ____ No
   If no, then when were you a resident of a nursing facility?_____
4. Are you on a special diet?   ____ Yes   ____ No
5. What percentage of your care is paid directly by you or your family?
   ____ 0%   ____1%–20%   ____21%–50%   ____ 51%–99%   ____ 100%

For Family/Friends Only

Please furnish the following information about yourself, and respond to the four statements located at the end of the survey.

1. The resident is my ____ Mother ____ Father ____ Wife ____ Husband
   ____ Brother ____ Sister ____ Friend ____ Other (explain)_____
   _____

2. How long has it been since you visited the facility?
   ____ Within the last week ____ Within the last month ____ Within the last 3 months
   ____ Within the last 6 months ____ Within the last year ____ More than 1 year ago

3. You are ____Male ____ Female

4. Your age is ____ 20–35 years ____ 36–45 years, ____ 46–55 years
   ____ 56–65 years ____ 66–75 years ____ Other (under 20 or more than 75)

5. Length of time your family member/friend has lived in the facility: ____ 0–6 months
   ____ 7–11 months ____ 1–3 years ____ 4–6 years ____ More than 7 years

6. What is your yearly household income?
   ____ Below $10,000 ____ $10,000–$25,000 ____ $25,001–$40,000
   ____ $40,001–$65,000 ____$65,001–$80,000 ____More than $80,000

7. What is the highest level of education you have achieved?
   ____ Elementary school ____Junior high (middle) school ____High school
   ____Some college ____College graduate ____ Graduate or postgraduate?

8. What percentage of the total nursing care costs is provided by you or your relative?
   ____ 0% ____ 1%–20% ____ 21%–50%
   ____ 51%–99% ____ 100% ____ Don't know

Please answer the following statements in a way that best sums up your opinion. For example, if you agree strongly with a given statement, then circle the number 1; if you have no particular opinion about a statement, then circle the number 3.

In my opinion . . .	Strongly Agree	Agree	Neutral	Disagree	Strongly disagree
1. Staff are sensitive to the needs of my family/friends.	1	2	3	4	5
2. Updated reports of my loved one's condition are provided consistently.	1	2	3	4	5
3. Staff communicate well with my family/friend/loved one.	1	2	3	4	5
4. Staff are honest and direct in their communications with my family/friend/loved one.	1	2	3	4	5

Family Satisfaction Opinion Survey—Abbey View Nursing Facility

The Family Satisfaction Opinion Survey was developed and administered by a consultant team at Abbey View Nursing Facility. Survey results were analyzed using a number of statistical tools, some of which are summarized here. Key findings at Abbey View are reported at the conclusion of this appendix. In addition, there is a description of the process used to administer the survey, which may highlight some issues to consider in planning a survey process.

Family Satisfaction Opinion Survey

We are conducting a survey to measure your satisfaction with Abbey View Nursing Facility. Please answer the following questions by placing a check mark in the appropriate column or by writing in the appropriate answer. Space is provided at the bottom of the survey for additional comments you would like to make.

	Very good 5	Good 4	Neutral 3	Poor 2	Very poor 1	N/A 0
Overall satisfaction						
Care, therapy, food, facility, activities, administration						
Services provided met with expectations						
Care and therapy						
Quality of nursing care						
Quality of care delivered by nursing assistants						
Treatment of family by staff						
Attention to appearance and personal care						
Provision for privacy and dignity						
Quality of occupational, physical, and/or speech therapy						
Delivery of information about resident's condition prompt						
Accuracy of information about resident's condition						
Opportunity for family's involvement in care planning						
Food						
Quality						
Dining environment						
Facility						
Air quality (odors, temperature)						
Cleanliness						
General maintenance						
Attention to safety						
Directional signs for visitors						
Security of personal property						
Activities						
Availability of for residents						
Encouragement for residents to join in						
Opportunities for family members to participate						
Administration						
Quality of admissions process (efficiency, comfort)						
Experience with senior staff						
Experience with Business Office						
Answers to questions/concerns provided						

Resident Demographic Information

Level of care (circle one):   First floor   Second floor   Third floor
Sex (circle one):   Male   Female
Age: ____
Length of residence in facility: ____ years, ____ months

Your Comments

_____

_____

_____

Thank you very much for your input. We will share the results of our survey with all residents and family members. If you want to be contacted personally, you may provide the information below.

Name of resident: _____

Your name: _____

Your address: _____

Your daytime telephone number (including area code): _____

About the Abbey View Family Satisfaction Survey

We introduced you to Abbey View Nursing Facility and its Family Satisfaction Survey in Chapter 6. A survey team conducted the survey there and analyzed the results using several statistical measures. The intent of the Family Satisfaction Survey is to collect and understand the opinions of the family/caretakers/significant friends (FCF) customer group. Results are then used by the facility for corrective action as well as in strategic planning and marketing. It also is important to measure the current level of performance in order to provide baseline comparisons at regular future intervals.

About Abbey View Nursing Facility

The organization described in the statistical study is one facility in a national group. Abbey View's residents are primarily frail older adults who are no longer able to care for themselves independently. They require varying degrees of nursing care, as indicated by the three residence floor units. First-floor residents are high functioning and independent and require less skilled nursing care than do the residents of other floors. Second-floor residents display cognitive and behavioral impairments, such as dementia or Alzheimer's disease, so they require some skilled nursing care. Third-floor residents require the most skilled nursing care for a variety of medical conditions; residents often display multiple medical problems. They may be temporary residents in need of subacute care after hospital stays.

In October 1994 the facility's ending census was 173 residents, with approximately 40% each on the second and third floors and 20% on the first floor. Of all residents, 79% were female. The families of all residents received the survey.

Survey Process

In order to boost the percentage of returned surveys, the consulting team sent the survey with a cover letter from the facility's administrator and a stamped return envelope. The advantage of returning surveys to a different, neutral location was discussed by the team and the facility's administrator. The team decided that there was a greater advantage to posting several collection boxes at locations around the facility, where FCFs would be visiting anyway. Reminder postcards were sent to all of the families 1 week before the due date.

Importance of Measuring Family Satisfaction. FCFs are considered the primary customers of nursing facilities, along with the residents, because many residents can no longer live alone or make decisions independently. Therefore, the Family Satisfaction Survey that was developed for Abbey View addresses the needs and perceptions of this particular FCF customer group. Response data were analyzed for counts, means (averages), and percentages.

Summary of Survey Results

There were 26 variables included on the survey, grouped into 6 areas: overall satisfaction, care and therapy, food, facility, activities, and administration. Through statistical analysis (multiple regression), the team showed that the best predictors of family satisfaction included 5 of the 26 component variables:

- Quality of nursing care
- Quality of care delivered by nursing assistants
- Provision for privacy and dignity
- Air quality
- Prompt delivery of information about resident's condition

It was shown statistically that of the 26 variables surveyed, these 5 factors explained 66.4% of FCFs' overall satisfaction. Four of the five factors fall into the care and therapy (i.e., interpersonal) area of the survey and therefore are within control of the facility and its staff. Studies in the professional literature confirm that the quality of the interpersonal relationships of staff with residents and family members/caregivers has most impact on customer satisfaction.[2] Other summary information is found in the paragraphs that follow and in Chapter 6.

Management Summary of Key Statistical Results

Scale: 5 (very good) → 3 (neutral) → 1 (very poor)

Total responses: 90 surveys received, 74 usable for statistical tests due to omitted responses; all 90 considered in open-ended comments analysis

Overall family satisfaction: 4.2
   Average, first floor: 4.35
   Average, second floor: 4.12
   Average, third floor: 4.25

Abbey View met my expectations: 4.1

Key components of overall satisfaction*
   Quality of nursing care: 4.3
   Quality of care delivered by nursing assistants: 4.0
   Provision for privacy and dignity: 4.0
   Delivery of information about resident prompt: 4.3
   Air quality: 3.8

Demographics
   Average length of stay: 3.0 years
   Average age: 84.1 years
   Percentage female: 79%
   Means for all component factors: low 3.4, high 4.4
   Standard deviations for all component factors: low .5, high 1.1

Open-Ended Comments from Survey (Qualitative Data)

Open-ended comments supplement and humanize the statistical data on survey responses. These data reflect individual customers' voices, separate from the aggregated data totals or statistical summaries. The data on open-ended comments from Abbey View are reprinted in the table on page 149. These open-ended verbal comments are clustered into families of related topics, then further segmented, and, finally, totaled. All of the open-ended comments are reported here verbatim. The complaints logged were found to be similar to other facilities and reports in the literature; they signaled areas that required attention in order to improve resident care and satisfy family members. The comments from Abbey View were grouped for analysis and reported to management as follows.

Overall Family Satisfaction. Many comments were very warm and appreciative. For example, "We are very happy with Mom's care and feels she gets loving personal attention. We would recommend the facility to anyone." There was a high proportion of positive comments in this general area; only 2% of the comments were negative regarding overall satisfaction, which supports the findings of overall satisfaction from the 26 questions.

Critical Comments. Most of the other open-ended comments are negative, which probably illustrates a desire to be helpful, to improve resident care, or to release stressful feelings in family members; the comments did not seem to be highly critical, however. Basic overall satisfaction with Abbey View and meeting customer expectations confirm this broad assessment. (Marketing research has shown that a customer who is satisfied after a problem is settled is more loyal than a customer who never had a problem at all.)

Segmentation of the data by floor allows staff to address problems that trouble particular family members the most:

   Attention given to appearance and personal care, second and third floors
   Nursing assistants, first and third floors

---

*Using several statistical tests, these five component statistics were compared across floor units (care levels) against overall satisfaction to understand how closely they determined overall satisfaction.

Food, first and third floors
Odors, especially second floor
Security of personal property and laundry, second and third floors
Activities, third floor

Care and Therapy. The open-ended comments were numerous and mostly critical and/or helpful. The survey team believes that this area reflects the central concern of most of the FCF group. The staff could focus improvement projects in this interpersonal area.

Facility. A number of negative comments showed that family members were aware of the physical upkeep and security issues that were listed in the survey.

Communications. Thoughtful and considered responses were offered; FCFs obviously were glad to be asked. The staff should reach out more often to family members who do not complain or speak up; for example: "We are really up in the air as to Joseph's condition. We haven't asked, but hope for information."

Surveys Containing No Verbal Comments. A large proportion of responses with no added verbal comments were attributed to all floors. The second-floor percentage was especially high (58%), perhaps because there is the smallest likelihood of potential future improvement with these residents, who are cognitively and behaviorally impaired.

Future Surveys

Abbey View administration may want to resurvey some areas in the future because of the first survey's small sample size. To gauge improvement longitudinally, the survey team should question the group again in a year or two—sooner if process improvements are made. Resurveys confirm results and help establish causal factors.

Family Survey Responses: Open-Ended Comments

Contributing open-ended comments was optional on the Abbey View survey. Comments were analyzed in two ways: positive and negative responses analyzed by floor unit, per general area of interest (e.g., care and therapy), and negative responses only on some specific issues analyzed by floor unit. Staff should be able to take action in response, particularly concerning specific problems on floors.

Category	*First floor (18)* Positive	Negative	*Second floor (36)* Positive	Negative	*Third floor (36)* Positive	Negative
Overall family satisfaction	6	—	8	2	7	—
Care and therapy	2	4	1	12	—	20
Personal appearance/care	—	1	—	7	—	5
Nursing assistants	—	3	—	3	—	8
Prompt, accurate information	—	1	—	1	—	—
Nursing care	—	—	—	2	—	4
Food	—	2	—	1	1	5
Facility	2	4	—	10	1	13
Odor	—	1	—	7	—	2
Security	—	—	—	5	—	5
Safety	—	1	—	1	—	—
Cleanliness	—	1	—	1	—	4
Activities	—	—	—	2	—	5
Administration	—	—	—	—	—	—
No comments	2 (11%)		21 (58%)		13 (36%)	

Note: Five responses did not designate a floor unit, so they were omitted from the totals. The total number of surveys are contained in parentheses in the column heads.

For the Data Lovers Among Us

The survey team's intent was to develop and administer a customer satisfaction survey for the FCFs of long-term care facility residents. Because so often the residents are frail older adults who can no longer live or make decisions independently, the FCFs are considered, along with residents, the primary customers of nursing facilities. The Family Satisfaction Survey developed for Abbey View addresses the needs and perceptions of this particular FCF customer group.

The survey compared the degree of satisfaction of family members of residents across three different levels of nursing care (three floor units) at the facility. It also examined 26 variables that were judged to be the most important in determining overall total customer satisfaction by using three models of multiple regression analysis.

Summary of Survey Results. No significant differences across the three care levels of overall family/caregiver satisfaction were demonstrated by these data, testing at the 90% level of confidence. That care levels are so similar seems to indicate consistency in nursing care and other process variables throughout the facility across residence floor units. Based on these survey returns, the overall total satisfaction of the FCFs who responded was 4.2 on a Likert scale of 5 (5 = very good, 1 = very poor). Abbey View met the respondents' expectations at a 4.1 level on the Likert scale. The averages of the responses to all 26 questions were consistently in the "good" range; most of them were more than 4.

The professional literature has demonstrated that the opinions of the FCFs do not necessarily reflect the opinions of the residents. The survey team did not attempt to correlate families'/caregivers' responses with residents' opinions, however.

Consultants' Comments on Statistical Findings. Beyond the recommendations provided here, Abbey View's administration can consider the following:

- Quality of nursing care and prompt delivery of information regarding residents' conditions are highly correlated (0.762), probably because family members expect nurses to inform them about their loved one's condition or because nurses are the professionals with whom they meet most often.
- Family members also may expect nurses to control some factors that they cannot control, such as air quality. Nurses and nursing assistants should not be surprised when this happens.
- The team compared the professional literature and articles with the Abbey View survey results. Most sources reported demographic data that were similar to Abbey View's, so outcomes could be compared appropriately. Other researchers found that the interpersonal aspects of care are most highly correlated with overall satisfaction. They also found that overall satisfaction is highly correlated with recommending the facility to others, an important marketing consideration.
- One interesting comment from a family member addressed interpersonal priorities for many families: "We are so pleased with the care given Mother that we are willing to overlook the smell on her floor, which is so hard to prevent, and the fact that several of her dresses and sweaters have disappeared over time."[2]

References

1   Kleinsorge, I.K., & Koenig, H.F. (1991, December). The silent customer: Measuring customer satisfaction in nursing homes. *Journal of Health Care Marketing, 11*(4), 3.

2   Armstrong, 1994, p. 1 ff.

Appendix G
Preliminary Strategic Planning for QMI (Sample)

This document reports one organization's first try at strategic planning for QMI. It reflects the issues about which senior management was concerned.

Anticipated outcomes of successful QMI processes

Improved employee and customer satisfaction with quality outcomes
Improved processes that deliver effective health care and other services
Impressive cost savings for the organization
Employee involvement in continuous process improvement for both individuals and teams
Enhanced manager and supervisor effectiveness
Improved risk management through clear, timely warnings of potential process problems
Better record keeping practices that satisfy regulatory requirements and standards
Employee job satisfaction, with decrease in turnover

1. Current situation:
   - Customers/suppliers identified
   - Does organization now have a vision and mission?
   - Establish priorities in sequence of project and of strategic planning process
2. Probable numbers of staff and others to be involved:
   - Management team
   - Quality council or other quality management infrastructure to be established
   - Staff involvement in training, team problem-solving, and so forth
   - Will focus groups or task forces or teams include customer representatives, members of the Board of Trustees, or only employees of the organization?
3. Project activities to consider:
   - Overviews and other communications
   - Strategic planning with senior management and quality council
     - Consider using state quality award framework and training/site team
     - State quality framework is related to Malcolm Baldrige National Quality Award's 1999 health care criteria
   - Orientation, training, and consulting support for management and quality council
     - Attend focused additional training for senior managers? Key board members?
   - Training and education
   - Team formation and facilitation of process improvement activities
4. Implementation plans
   - QMI activities at all levels of organization reflect senior-level QMI vision and policies, guided by quality council
     - Each strategic objective selected to include measurable indicators of key processes
     - Should projects focus only on in-house processes or should they include suppliers/vendors and customers?
5. Resource allocation to initial phases of QMI
   - Probable time horizons for QMI process implementation: planning, initial training, and so forth

Appendix H
Omnibus Budget Reconciliation Act of 1987 (OBRA)

Background information on the Omnibus Budget Reconciliation Act of 1987 (OBRA) and the regulatory/survey process provides insight into the complex process that governs changes in regulatory requirements in health care and the long-term care industry.

Throughout all of these survey changes government regulations have shared certain goals. Government regulation of nursing facilities has two broad goals: 1) consumer protection, which ensures the safety of residents, the adequacy of care that they receive, and the protection of their legal rights; and 2) control of and accounting for the large public expenditures, chiefly Medicaid, that are used to pay for nursing care.[1] The changes required by OBRA '87 provided nursing facility reforms [that] largely were welcomed by providers, regulators, and advocates. The complexity of the process makes effective enforcement implementation potentially difficult.[2]

OBRA '87 marked a major shift in how states monitor the quality of the services offered by nursing facilities. Prior to implementing the reforms in October 1990, surveys of homes receiving Medicare or Medicaid funds stressed reviewing processes and records to document compliance with federal standards. The previous chart audit process was replaced by a "resident centered, outcome oriented" approach that allows observation of how well the staff meet individual resident assessed needs and how meaningfully the facility supports assessed resident well-being. This paradigm shift reflects the recommendations identified in the Institute of Medicine's (IoM) 1986 study, *Improving the Quality of Care in Nursing Homes.*[3]

The reforms addressed the problems that the IoM identified with the previous nursing facility survey process. The previous process included an annual survey, an annual inspection of the care provided to each Medicaid recipient (both utilization review and quality of care), and the ad hoc investigation of complaints. Among the problems that the IoM identified were survey timing predictability, focus on paper compliance, insensitivity to resident needs, and ease with which substandard facilities could avoid being terminated by maintaining compliance only long enough to become recertified.[4] OBRA established the requirements for minimum levels of quality standards in resident rights, resident behavior and facility practices, quality of nursing care and rehabilitation services, and quality of life in skilled nursing facilities (SNFs) and nursing facilities (NFs) participating in Medicare and Medicaid programs.

The survey team plays an important role in survey and compliance citation decision making. The determination of a citation that triggers enforcement penalties must be accurate and consistent.[5] . . . [Thus] enforcement regulations are directed toward those facilities that frequently go in and out of compliance.[6]

References

1   Stoil, referenced in Erickson, J.M. (1994). *Level A compliance decision making report.* Washington, DC: Foundation of the American College of Health Care Administrators.

2   Ibid., p. 15.

3   Ibid., p. 1.

4   Ibid., p. 4.

5   Ibid., p. 1.

6   Ibid., p. 4.

Appendix I
QMI Needs Assessment Interview on Current Status of Facility

This document may be adapted as necessary for initial QMI needs assessments with the facility's administrator. This initial interview allows the person who is facilitating the QMI process to gain a foundational knowledge of the current understanding and beliefs regarding quality management.

Administrator Interview

Length of service at this facility:

Services offered (e.g., dementia, subacute, other special programming):

Organizational structure:

Strengths of facility:

Opportunities for improvements in facility:

Most pressing quality issues:

Knowledge of/background in QMI:

Attitude toward QMI:

Department heads' knowledge/background in QMI:

Department heads' attitude toward QMI:

Synergy of department management team:

General response of staff to change initiatives:

Quality assessment and assurance committee:
Who is on the committee:

Frequency of meetings:

Effectiveness of committee:

Current quality assurance plan:

Medical Director:
Level of involvement:

Openness to QMI:

Data collection and analysis systems:

Training processes:

Director of Nursing/Quality Coordinator Interview

Length of service at this facility:

Strengths of facility:

Opportunities for improvements in facility:

Most pressing quality issues:

Feedback mechanisms available:

Appendix J
For Further Reading and
Viewing—QMI at the Library

Many seminars and books provide detail on QMI tools and techniques. The QMI tools themselves are generic, although they are easier to learn when examples and vocabulary deal specifically with health care. This list includes many personal favorites, both within and outside health care. Many are available through public library or university systems. Additional resources are listed in the Bibliography. Although health care professionals often turn to general resources, coverage of CQI/TQM for health care delivery, specifically for long-term care delivery, is expanding quickly.

Books

Albin, J.M. (1992). *Quality improvement in employment and other human services: Managing for quality through change.* Baltimore: Paul H. Brookes Publishing Co.
Excellent discussion of QMI processes, with clear descriptions and examples of a great number of quality management tools, including the seven quality control tools and the seven quality management tools; a fine resource

Berwick, D.M., A.B. Godfrey, & J. Roessner. (1990). *Curing health care—New strategies for quality improvement.* San Francisco: Jossey-Bass.
Contains an excellent appendix that illustrates and explains the CQI/TQM tools and several health care case studies

Brassard, M., & D. Ritter. (1994). *The memory jogger II: A pocket guide of tools for continuous improvement and effective planning.* Methuen, MA: GOAL/QPC. [Tel.: 800-643-4316]
A pocket-size textbook that highlights CQI tools and team techniques; GOAL/QPC has added many "Memory Jogger" supplementary training materials

Byham, W.C., et al. (1993). *Zapp! Empowerment in health care.* New York: Fawcett Columbine Publishers.
A delightful fable for frontline supervisors in health care, illustrating the power and possible barriers of employee involvement; a very effective tool in training supervisors

Caldwell, C. (1995). *Mentoring strategic change in health care: An action guide.* Milwaukee: American Society for Quality/Quality Press. [Tel.: 800-248-1946]
Caldwell provides many implementable tools, along with inspiration for senior executive leadership; he explains his transformation model for TQM with a multitude of examples, many from the health care environment; emphasizes the senior manager's role in TQM/CQI

CARF (The Rehabilitation Accreditation Commission), Employment and Community Services Division. (1997). *Managing outcomes: Customer-driven outcomes measurement & management systems.* Tucson, AZ: Author.
A guide to development and use of an organizational measurement and outcomes management system based on customer needs and an effective 6-step process for managing QMI systems and processes

Elzey, F.F. (1974). *A first reader in statistics* (2nd ed). Belmont, CA: Brooks/Cole.
A clear, logical, and very readable introduction to statistical definitions and concepts

Fink, A., & J. Kosecoff. (1985). *How to conduct surveys: A step-by-step guide.* Beverly Hills, CA: Sage Publications.
A guide to developing and administering surveys; includes a section on statistical analysis of survey results

Gonick, L., & W. Smith. (1993). *The cartoon guide to statistics.* New York: HarperCollins.
A truly painless introduction to basic statistical concepts (Imagine laughing at a statistical definition!)

Greeley, H.P., & J.I. Cofer. (1993). *Quality improvement techniques for long-term care.* Marblehead, MA: Opus Communications. [Tel.: 617-639-0033]
Good guide to beginning the quality journey; simple illustrations are easy to follow and understand; good reference material for trainers

Hayes, B.E. (1992). *Measuring customer satisfaction: Development and use of questionnaires.* Milwaukee: ASQ Quality Press. [Tel.: 800-248-1946]
A classic in the field of developing and using surveys; clear definitions and descriptions of key scientific principles and vocabulary that relate to surveys and customer satisfaction

Joiner, B.L. (1994). *Fourth generation management: The new business consciousness.* New York: McGraw-Hill.
Focuses on quality improvement, managing quality, and how to structure successful organizations; *"How the evolution of management and the revolution in quality are converging, and what it means for business [or health care] and the nation"*

Juran, J.M. (1989). *Juran on leadership for quality—An executive handbook.* New York: The Free Press.
Juran describes effective leadership goals and techniques for organization transformation.

Juran, J.M., & Gryna, F. (1993). *Quality planning and analysis: From product development through use* (3rd ed.). New York: McGraw-Hill.

LaVigna, G.W., et al. (1994). *The periodic service review: A total quality assurance system for human services and education.* Baltimore: Paul H. Brookes Publishing Co.
Many good examples of procedures and formats for implementing QMI; a very straightforward approach to health care supervision

Lawton, R.L. (1991). *Creating a customer-centered culture: For service-quality leadership.* Bloomington, MN: Training Materials.

Leebov, W., & C.J. Ersoz. (1991). *The health care manager's guide to continuous quality improvement.* Chicago: American Hospital Publishing.
An excellent resource for health care process improvement, with many examples of the CQI/TQM tools in use, particularly in hospitals; a section called "The Manager's Tool Kit" illustrates applications of TQM team techniques, charting key indicators, and so forth

Scholtes, P.R., et al. (1988). *The team handbook.* Madison, WI: Joiner Associates. [Tel.: 800-669-8326]
Straightforward, user-friendly guidelines for both teams and managers on data collection implementation and successful team activities

Stoesz, E., & C. Raber. (1994). *Doing good better: How to be an effective board member.* Intercourse, PA: Good Books Publishers.
A clear and simple discussion of board members' "dos and don'ts"; clear, direct discussion of this important leadership role; clarifies differences from administration and operations responsibilities

Stofac, T.J. (1994). *Continuous quality initiatives: A manager's guide.* Des Moines, IA: Briggs Corporation.
A workbook that guides implementation of TQM/CQI processes and change in corporate culture

Walton, M. (1986). *The Deming management method.* New York: Putnam.
A description of Deming's work and philosophy, in many ways more readable and compact than his own books; foreword by Deming

Journal Articles

American Association of Homes and Services for the Aging. (1997, January). AAHSA's MDS-based quality improvement system. *Nursing Homes,* 23–26.

Anonymous. (1998, December). Changing your way of thinking just might solve the CNA crisis. *Briefings on Long-Term Care Regulations,* 1–2.

Chaufournier, R.L., & C. St. Andre. (1993, April). Total quality management in an academic health center. *Quality Progress,* 63–66.

Cooper, J. (1996, Winter). Long-term care should attempt to embrace total quality management. *Journal of Long-Term Care Administration,* 15–16.

Dewey, J. (1994, October). Driving quality. *Provider,* 38–42.

Ditulio, T. (1998, September). Getting dementia patients to sparkle. *Nursing Homes,* 41–42.

Dugan, J. (1996, Winter). Is total quality management a savvy trend or managerial trap? *Journal of Health Care Administration,* 5–8.

Fishpaw, R. (1996, Winter). Total quality management benefits nursing homes. *Journal of Long-Term Care Administration,* 9–13.

Fitzgerald, R.P., B.N. Shiverick, & D. Zimmerman. (1996). Applying performance measures to long term care. *Journal on Quality Improvement, 22*(7), 505–517.

Fronheiser, L.P. (1998, April). PPS's $1,500 cap—Hope for the best ... plan for the worst. *Nursing Homes,* 22–27.

Hyde, J., J. Hillygus, B. Levy, & S. Levkoff. (1998, September/October). Using outcome measures to provide excellence in Alzheimer care. *American Journal of Alzheimer's Disease,* 265–272.

Kane, R., M. Maciejewski, & M. Finch. The relationship of patient satisfaction with care and clinical outcomes. *Medical Care, 35*(7), 714–730.

Kindrat, T. (1995, September–October). Directions: Measuring quality in long term care. *Leadership, 4*(5), 33–35.

King, C.A. (1985, June). Service quality assurance is different. *Quality Progress,* 14–18.

Klitch, B.A. (1997, November/December). Quality indicators: The new survey tool. *Nursing Homes,* 9–10.

Larson, E.R. (1998, November). An era of positive change: The Baldrige Award's future. *Quality Digest,* 28–31.

Lawton, R.L. (1991, September). Creating a customer-centered culture in service industries. *Quality Progress,* 69–72.

March, T. (1998, November). Profiting from patience: TQM pays off. *Quality Digest,* 40–42.

McCullough et al. (1993). Mapping personal, familial, and professional values in long-term care decisions. *Gerontologist, 33*(3), 324–332.

Morrison, M.H. (1998, April). Adapting to PPS—The business realities. *Nursing Homes,* 12–16.

Norton, P.G., et al. (1996). Satisfaction of residents and families in long-term care. I: Construction and application of an instrument. *Quality Management in Health Care, 4*(3), 38–46.

Pecora, P.J., R. Massinga, & H. Mauzerall. (1997, April). Measuring outcomes in the changing environment of child welfare services. *Child and Family Focus,* 2–6.

Popejoy, M. (1996, Winter). The drawbacks of TQM programs in long-term care. *Journal of Long-Term Care Administration,* 14.

Quality assessment and improvement for Medicaid managed care. (1996, Summer). *Health Care Financing Review, 17*(4), 97–115.

Ramsay, J., F. Sainfort, & D. Zimmerman. (1995). An empirical test of the structure, process and outcome quality paradigm using resident-based, nursing facility assessment data. *American Journal of Medical Quality, 10*(2), 63–75.

Ready, set, automate! (1998, January). *Nursing Homes,* 41–44.

Reinertsen, J.L., (1993). Outcomes management and continuous quality improvement: The compass and the rudder. *Quality Review Bulletin, 19*(1), 5–7.

Sainfort, F., J. Ramsay, P. Ferreira, & L. Mezghani. (1994). A first step in total quality management of nursing facility care: Development of an empirical model of structure, process, and outcome dimensions. *American Journal of Medical Quality, 9*(2), 75–86.

Simmons, S.F., J.F. Schnelle, & A.N. Rahman. (1998, June). How "real" is your resident satisfaction survey? *Nursing Homes,* 60–63.

Smith, J. (1998, May). Refocusing the nursing staff for PPS success. *Nursing Homes,* 18–25.

Soberman, L.R., et. al. (1997). Satisfaction of residents and families in long-term care. III: Dissemination of results. *Quality Management in Health Care, 5*(3), 63–71.

Van Maris, B., et al., Satisfaction of residents and families in long-term care. II: Lessons that we learned. *Quality Management in Health Care, 4*(3), 47–53.

Zastowny, T., W. Stratmann, E. Adams, & M. Fox. (1995). Patient satisfaction and experience with health services and quality of care. *Quality Management in Health Care, 3*(3), 50–61.

Zinn, J., D. Brannon, & V. Mor. Organizing for nursing home quality. *Quality Management in Health Care, 3*(4), 37–46.

Other Resources

American Society for Quality (ASQ), Milwaukee, WI. [Tel.: 800-248-1946]
Professional organization dedicated to quality management; monthly meetings in various state sections; excellent monthly national journal; economical cost; national ASQ has a health care division; administers the Malcolm Baldrige National Quality Awards for the (U.S.) National Institute of Standards and Technology

Institute for Healthcare Improvement (IHI). Boston, MA. [Tel.: 617-754-4800]
A nonprofit organization designed to be a major force for integrative and collaborative efforts to accelerate improvement in health care systems; offers CQI training, which is particularly successful with senior managers; also offers "Breakthrough Series Collaboratives," which facilitate regional and national networking between organizations to accelerate improvement processes in all attendees

Malcolm Baldrige National Quality Award. [Tel.: 301-975-2036, fax: 301-948-3716, email: nqp@nist.gov]
Baldrige Criteria for Performance Excellence provides quality management guidelines in all types of organizations; can be used to guide organization's self-assessment; any group can implement the guidelines successfully as frameworks for total quality integration, without planning to apply for the award; after 1999 award cycle, health care and education each considered separately from other for-profit and not-for-profit industries; note that the MBNQA framework has been improved periodically since 1988; single copies of the framework are free

State quality awards
Like the Baldrige award, the quality frameworks may be used without applying for awards; some at the state level include government organizations; a number of states provide quality training and mentoring services

Mor, V. *Do Good Nursing Homes Provide Good Care?* National Institute on Aging Grant No. R37 AG11624, 1994.

The Parkview Experience. (Distributed by Excellence in Training Corporation [Tel.: 800-747-6569].)
An excellent video about a hospital's implementation of quality management techniques, particularly useful for senior health care managers and teams

Tools for Continual Improvement. (Distributed by Executive Learning, Inc. [Tel.: 800-929-7890].)
An excellent series of videos demonstrating application of many CQI/TQM tools in different health care settings, with real-life scenarios

Appendix K
Accelerators and Inhibitors Require Quality Council's Attention

Accelerators and inhibitors to organization transformation enhance the activities of the quality council and guide senior management in implementing QMI. According to Caldwell,[1] quality councils invest great numbers of resources in accelerating changes in processes and policies; however, he believes that an equal or greater investment in eliminating inhibitors would be more effective. These guidelines may be helpful in strategizing an organization's approach to change in corporate culture. (They are part of Caldwell's organizational transformation model, reflecting the concepts of Lewin and Senge's reinforcing model for a learning organization.)

Accelerators of Quality Transformation and Innovation

Make heroes of champions and producers.
Link the TQM quality plan to the accomplishment of strategic plans.
Promote a shared vision.
Focus on measurement.
Assign meaningful work.
Create constant discomfort with the current state.
Make sure that senior management is visible.
Maintain momentum (e.g., storyboards, storyboard reviews, team road maps).
Network with other TQM organizations.
Build the self-esteem of every employee and manager to participate in vision achievement.
Remember the quality council's accelerators.
Spend at least 50% of the quality council's time on achieving results.
Spend at least 40% of the quality council's time on resolving infrastructure issues (e.g., performance appraisal process, organizational structure).
Adopt a mental model of the transformation process, and broadcast it to employees.
Conduct an annual Baldrige Award type of self-assessment, and revise the strategic deployment road map to include recommendations.
Assign a sponsor from the quality council to each quality improvement team, quality planning team, and business process quality management team.
Conduct an annual cost-of-poor-quality study, and use the results to drive team chartering.
Use TQM tools and methods (e.g., flowcharts) to draw policies and procedures.

Inhibitors to Be Neutralized

The following categories, if neutralized, enable the accelerators to achieve maximum effectiveness. Their importance often is underestimated by organization leaders, who tend to focus on accelerator issues.

Lack of employee empowerment
Socializing champions (directing the attention of effective individuals to secondary activities [e.g., facilitation, aid to colleagues, presentations] rather than focusing on active process improvement)
Paradigm lock (i.e., inability to innovate)
Lack of structure
Organizational design flaws
Constantly changing TQM policy

Proceeding without evidence of readiness

Senior management's impatience with department heads (overemphasis on immediate results, impatience with managers as they learn to apply TQM methods)

Failure to recognize and confront failures

Variation in skills and leadership abilities

Focusing improvement initiatives on "bad apples" (using data as a judgment tool rather than for improvement or learning)[2]

References

1   Caldwell, C. (1995). *Mentoring strategic change in health care: An action guide* (pp. 151–153). Milwaukee: American Society for Quality/Quality Press.

2   Ibid.

Appendix L
Quality Management Plan (Sample)

(_____)

Name of Facility

This sample plan provides a framework for describing the structure, function, and processes of the organization's quality management system. Many other versions are acceptable. This plan assumes that the organization's former quality assurance committee has been developed to include continuous quality improvement principles.

Purpose

(Statement of the purpose of quality management in the facility as well as how it aligns with the facility's mission and values.)

Objectives

The objectives of quality management are

- To create an organizational environment that supports the fulfillment of the facility's mission and vision of quality care and service
- To ensure that customers' expectations are being identified and met
- To support continuous improvement and innovation through the involvement of employees at all levels

Quality Council Structure

The (_____) quality council is responsible for the administration of the facility's quality management process. The administrator is the council's chairperson, and the quality coordinator is the council's facilitator. Quality council membership may include representatives from the following departments:

Nursing (DON, at minimum)

Social Services

Recreation Therapy

Rehabilitation Therapy

Environmental Services
Dietary Services
Pharmacy Services
Business Office
Medical Services (Medical Director or an attending physician)

HCFA requires, at minimum, the Director of Nursing, the physician designated by the facility, and at least three facility staff members to participate in the quality assessment and assurance (QA&A) group. The membership of the quality council may or may not be the same as that of the QA&A committee. Some facilities may prefer having a small quality council that guides the QMI process through senior department heads.

Quality Council Accountability

The (_____) quality council is accountable for maintaining and improving facility systems that result in high-quality care and service to customers. The quality council oversees all quality-related activities within the facility and is responsible for coordinating these activities among and between problem-solving groups. This oversight enables the council to recognize interrelationships among the groups and to make appropriate connections and communication that result in efficiency and effectiveness in the facility's problem-solving efforts.

The quality council establishes and maintains systems that provide two-way communication with facility staff for the purpose of keeping them informed about the activities of and the progress made by the quality council and of obtaining input from staff regarding current or potential quality issues. The quality council oversees the work of process improvement teams as well as permanent committees, including the

Infection control committee
Risk management committee
Ethics committee
Policy committee

Process improvement teams and ongoing committees receive direction from the quality council. Through the use of charters, the quality council defines clear expectations, boundaries, and resources that are available to the groups. These problem-solving teams document their improvement processes and report their progress on tasks to the council on at least a quarterly basis.

The quality coordinator maintains documentation on all quality management activities. Such documentation includes the minutes of each meeting, data analysis summaries, and charters and their outcomes.

Quality Council Functions

The (_____) quality council meets at least monthly to carry out the following functions:

1. Define and communicate (_____'s) vision of high-quality care and service.
2. Identify and monitor facility systems and key processes that have an impact on the quality of care and service.
3. Define standards of care and service along with measurable indicators.
4. Develop systems that ensure continual assessment of customer needs and expectations.
5. Monitor key quality outcomes and customer satisfaction indices.
6. Prioritize and coordinate quality improvement efforts.
   - Charter projects for interdepartmental quality improvement teams
   - Approve the selection of team leaders and team facilitators (team leaders provide overall direction for the team; facilitators guide the improvement process)
   - Demonstrate visible support for teams, and provide guidance and assistance as necessary

- Approve recommendations and provide authority and resources for implementation
- Develop a tracking system for monitoring the results of team solutions
7. Develop and implement recognition processes that support the values of the organization.

Quality Council Methodology

Data Collection

The quality council develops a data collection system that supplies continual feedback regarding customer satisfaction and quality outcomes.

Customer Satisfaction Data

Customer satisfaction data are collected to understand customer opinions and concerns. This information is then used to prioritize and focus the improvement process.

Resident and family satisfaction surveys

Resident and family councils

Discharged resident satisfaction surveys

State/federal survey results—all survey and complaint information

Clinical Data

Clinical data are collected routinely and analyzed to determine patterns, trends, and unacceptable outcomes. Data include problems or risks that may cause harm or violate residents' rights, such as the following:

- Incidence of new fractures
- Prevalence of falls
- Prevalence of behavioral symptoms affecting others
- Prevalence of depressive symptoms
- Use of nine or more different medications
- Incidence of cognitive impairment
- Prevalence of fecal or urinary incontinence
- Prevalence of indwelling catheters
- Prevalence of fecal impaction
- Prevalence of tube feeding
- Prevalence of dehydration
- Prevalence of bedbound residents
- Incidence of decline in activities of daily living
- Incidence of decline in range of motion
- Prevalence of antipsychotics use, in the absence of psychotic and related conditions
- Prevalence of antianxiety/hypnotic use
- Prevalence of daily physical restraints
- Prevalence of little or no activity
- Prevalence of Stages 1–4 pressure ulcers

Human Resources Data

Human resources data are collected to understand employee attitudes and concerns. The indicators chosen will focus department team efforts in areas such as hiring and firing and will track progress toward improvement goals.

Employee satisfaction surveys

Employee exit interviews

Employee incidents

Employee turnover rate

Financial Data
>   Census by payer type
>   Pool usage
>   Case mix
>   Staff ratios per resident per day
>   Therapy units
>   Accounts receivable
>   Diagnosis (Dx) and length of stay (LOS) of subacute residents

Data Analysis

Quality Council

All outcomes data are analyzed by the quality council or the quality council's subcommittee to identify patterns and trends. This information is used to prioritize improvement efforts and to generate ideas for innovation. Retrospective reviews on abnormal findings are conducted to determine root causes and to draw out key things that have been learned that can be applied facility-wide to prevent problems and reinforce the continual learning concept of the QMI model.

Reports of key indicators are examined at regular intervals and are used to benchmark the facility's data against those of other facilities. Indicators may be chosen from collected Minimum Data Set data, incidents or costs per resident per day indicators, other sources of electronically submitted data, and in-house data. Caution should be exercised when using Online Survey Certification and Reporting System (OSCAR) data, which are collected when surveyors first enter a facility. Because these data reflect only data that are collected within the first hour or so of facility inspection, accuracy and detail often are lacking in the OSCAR reports.

Process Improvement Teams

The data that are generated by the facility's process improvement teams are analyzed by the teams themselves. The information obtained is used to improve the process under study.

Departments

Within individual departments, monitoring systems are in place that detect unacceptable variations in key processes.

Process Improvement

The quality council charters improvement projects based on identified priorities. Charters include a clear statement of purpose, boundaries of the process to be studied, and the resources available. Process improvement teams (inter- or intradepartmental) are established to study and improve processes. Teams comprise individuals who work within the process being studied. Process improvement teams utilize the Plan–Do–Study–Act (PDSA; see Chapter 2) problem-solving method and maintain records of their activities. Routine, at least quarterly, communication exists between the process improvement teams and the quality council regarding the team's progress. Recommended improvement actions are reviewed and approved by the quality council. Improvement actions are communicated to affected individuals and groups, appropriate training/education is conducted, and the improvement actions are implemented. The quality council is responsible for establishing systems that sustain improvement efforts. The quality council retains records of process improvement team meetings, data collection and analysis, and improvement activities. These records are confidential, except as required by law.

Evaluation

The quality council evaluates improvement efforts and identifies the need for further action. The quality plan is reviewed annually and revised as necessary.

Appendix M
Assessment Tool for QMI Deployment
Strategic Planning for Organizational Development

The assessment tool for QMI deployment assesses the integration of all six core concepts of the QMI model (see Chapter 1). Each concept area includes some data-based assessment activities, which can be developed further. Using the following scale, circle the number that most accurately reflects the status of QMI within the facility.

3 = The standard is fully implemented.
2 = Most of the standard is implemented.
1 = Some of the standard is implemented.
0 = None of the standard is implemented.

After individuals have completed the assessment — in each department, for example — the quality council can use this tool to achieve consensus on priorities for the entire facility or corporate group.

Customer Focus

Our mission is communicated to our internal and external customers.	0	1	2	3
Our mission and commitment to our customers are communicated to those with whom we contract to serve our customers.	0	1	2	3
Customers receive information/education about the care and services we provide as well as how to contact the organization's leadership to share their ideas and concerns.	0	1	2	3
Job descriptions reflect accountability for the practice of positive customer relationships.	0	1	2	3
Employee performance evaluations include a measure of the employee's orientation toward customers.	0	1	2	3
Managers and supervisors are held accountable for modeling positive customer relationships.	0	1	2	3
We collect and analyze data regarding customer expectations and satisfaction with care and service (both internal and external customers).	0	1	2	3
Customer feedback (positive *and* negative) is shared with employees.	0	1	2	3
Improvement action plans are developed based on customer feedback.	0	1	2	3
Our process improvement system includes collecting data and responding to customers' complaints and employees' grievances.	0	1	2	3

Continual Learning

Our staff development program was designed to meet the organization's goals.	0	1	2	3
Potential employees are provided with an overview of our mission, vision, and quality management philosophy during the selection process.	0	1	2	3
New employees attend orientation activities and training about our quality management philosophy.	0	1	2	3
The effectiveness of the orientation process is tracked at periodic intervals.	0	1	2	3
During job-specific training, QMI principles are incorporated into all aspects of employees' daily work.	0	1	2	3
The learning needs and strengths of employees are assessed at the time of hire and are reassessed continuously to identify their ongoing training and education needs.	0	1	2	3

Employees receive a follow-up orientation within 4 months of hire to evaluate their progress and identify additional need for training.	0	1	2	3
Cross-training is encouraged.	0	1	2	3
Time is allocated for employees to attend continuing education programs.	0	1	2	3
Staff developers are skilled in training and communication methods and understand the principles of QMI.	0	1	2	3
Continual learning is promoted and supported by management.	0	1	2	3
A measurement system evaluates the impact of training and learning activities on employees.	0	1	2	3

Employee Involvement

An atmosphere of teamwork and trust exists within our organization.	0	1	2	3
Communication systems are open and inclusive and are aimed at reducing ambiguity and promoting healthy working relationships.	0	1	2	3
Employees are given the support and direction that they need to perform their jobs effectively.	0	1	2	3
Jobs are structured in a manner that promotes quality of work life:				
Involvement in problem solving and decision making	0	1	2	3
Ongoing positive and constructive feedback	0	1	2	3
Opportunities for growth and development	0	1	2	3
Support from supervisors and team members	0	1	2	3
Opportunities to use creativity and humor	0	1	2	3
Safe working conditions	0	1	2	3
Employees are held accountable for fostering an environment that demonstrates our value of workforce diversity.	0	1	2	3
Job descriptions and performance evaluations of supervisors reflect accountability for the practice of participative management.	0	1	2	3
We measure employee satisfaction and participation in continuous improvement activities.	0	1	2	3

Systems Orientation

Key organization systems are identified and communicated to staff.	0	1	2	3
Our communication systems are designed to optimize information sharing, mutual learning, and problem solving through the use of multiple communication methods.	0	1	2	3
Employees have access to the tools, equipment, and resources that are necessary to perform their jobs.	0	1	2	3
Cooperation and collaboration are promoted between individuals and departments.	0	1	2	3
We monitor changes in the external environment and initiate changes in our internal systems to meet customers' demands.	0	1	2	3
We clarify expectations with our suppliers and evaluate whether these expectations are met.	0	1	2	3
We measure the outcomes and processes of our key organization systems.	0	1	2	3

Continuous Process Improvement

Employees are involved in the continuous improvement of quality, including resolving existing problems, implementing process improvement ideas, and seeking innovative methods for delivering care and services.	0	1	2	3
Job descriptions include the expectation of employees' participation in QMI.	0	1	2	3
Employees are provided with basic, ongoing education that is related to QMI concepts and tools.	0	1	2	3
Staff are encouraged to contribute ideas for improvement in the organization.	0	1	2	3

Ongoing assessment and improvement of processes support steady
improvements in customer and employee satisfaction. 0 1 2 3
We use benchmarking as a source of measurement as well as to uncover
best practices. 0 1 2 3
QMI tools are used to maximize the efficiency and effectiveness of
processes and to promote quality outcomes. 0 1 2 3
Managers are evaluated on the extent to which they encourage and support
employee involvement in continuous improvement efforts. 0 1 2 3
We celebrate our improvement successes. 0 1 2 3
We measure supplier services and include supplier data in our process
improvement planning. 0 1 2 3
Data are collected and analyzed to determine patterns and trends, to
prioritize improvement efforts, and to generate ideas for innovation. 0 1 2 3

Leadership

Our senior staff understand their roles and are involved in transforming the
organization's culture. 0 1 2 3
Our organizational infrastructure supports QMI. 0 1 2 3
Our quality management plan clearly defines a system for identifying,
prioritizing, and resolving issues of quality. 0 1 2 3
Delivery of high-quality care and service is viewed as a top priority in our
organization. 0 1 2 3
Standards of quality care and service are based on customer expectations
and are regularly communicated to all employees. 0 1 2 3
We measure, evaluate, and communicate our success in meeting or
exceeding identified standards. 0 1 2 3
Employee contributions to QMI are recognized and communicated to all
employees. 0 1 2 3
Resources are allocated to prioritize and support our QMI initiatives. 0 1 2 3
We use pilot projects to test proposed solutions. 0 1 2 3
Our strategic plan considers both the external health care environment and
the strengths and weaknesses of the internal corporate environment. 0 1 2 3
Management decisions are based on data that have been collected and
analyzed. 0 1 2 3

Index

Page references followed by *f* or *t* indicate figures or tables, respectively.